Ocicat

The Ocicat Owner's Manual

Ocicat care, personality, grooming, health, training, costs and feeding all included.

By

Elliott Lang

Published by: IMB Publishing

Table of Contents

Acknowledgements

I wish to convey a special thanks to my family members who gave me the time and space I needed to write this book.

I would also like to pay special thanks to my friends and colleagues whose input proved valuable in obtaining all the necessary information I needed to develop the book.

Special thanks to the following organizations/associations for their valuable support:

The American Cat Fanciers Association (CFA)

America Pet Products Association

Cat Owners Association of Western Australia

The International Cat Association (TICA)

The Governing Council of the Cat Fancy (UK)

Pet Food Manufacturers Association (PFMA) – UK

American Animal Hospital Association (AAHA)

Worldwide Pet Owners Association

The Winn Feline Association

Ocicat Club (UK)

Ocicats of North America Club

OCIcat (Finland)

The Governing Council of the Cat Fancy of South Australia (GCCFSA)

Chapter 1 – Introduction

I have always been fascinated by different animals and cats in particular for the better part of my life. Having been brought up in a rural farm where my parents had different cat breeds, I developed a keen interest in cats, an interest that pushed me to want to know more about the different cat breeds, their origin and character among other issues.

My interest in cats has indeed been a long journey. Not only did I pick the habit of keeping cats as pets; I have over the years interacted and learnt valuable lessons from different cat breeders across the globe. Apart from the Abyssinian breed, the other cat breed that I came to develop a deep interest in is the Ocicat breed and in particular how it came to exist. This is one breed of cat that is not only friendly with owners and strangers alike; it gets along very well with other cats breeds, other pets such as dogs and children.

Different types of Ocicats are to be found, depending on spot colour. There are Chocolate, Silver, Lavender and Tawny spotted Ocicats. They are also sold at different prices depending on age, treatment and region.

Cat breeders in the USA for example sell registered, neutered/spayed and vaccinated Ocicat kittens at between $500 (£295and £593). Non-registered, non-neutered/spayed and non-vaccinated kittens go for between $300 and $800 (£177 and £474). Older Ocicats definitely cost more taking into account a breeder's expenses in taking care and maintenance.

The Ocicat is the cat of choice for anyone in need of a unique cat that presents the wild look associated with such wild animals as Leopards and Cheetahs yet with a friendly, domestic temperament. The Ocicat breed is no doubt one of the most popular cat breeds in the world. It is indeed found even in the remotest locations.

Chapter 2 – The Ocicat

History/Origin

"Even a mistake may turn out to be the one thing necessary for a worthwhile achievement." This famous quote by Henry Ford (1863-1947) aptly applies to the Ocicat, whose history and origin can be traced way back to 1964.

As part of her usual breeding program, Virginia Daly of Berkley, Michigan in the USA (a recognized cat breeder by Cat Fanciers Association) was out to develop a unique breed by cross-breeding a male Abyssinian cat with a female Siamese cat. The litter she obtained was indeed what she was looking for; Siamese kittens with Abyssinian features. A repeat of this breeding program, however, yielded a surprise result; an ivory kitten that featured golden spots, a kitten she named Tonga.

Although it was not her intention to develop a new breed, having got what she was out to get, she took care of Tonga, giving the kitten all the care and attention that it required. Her daughter, however, had a different view of Tonga. She had noted that Tonga was similar to Ocelot, the dwarf leopard native to South America. She therefore re-named the kitten Ocicat, giving birth to the now popular Ocicat.

Although developed by accident, the development of the Ocicat was a blessing to Daly. Because she could not use Tonga (now re-named Ocicat by her daughter) for further breeding, Daly repeated her "mistaken" breeding program and obtained other lovely Tawny-spotted kittens similar to Ocicat.

With an interest to develop a breed with unique bone features, she introduced the American Shorthair breed into her breeding program, this time obtaining kittens similar to the Ocicat but with silvery spots and strong bones.

Daly had to stop her breeding program soon after in 1966 when she was forced to sit back and care of her ailing mother. She had however registered her lovely Ocicat kittens through the Cat Fanciers Association.

It was until 1984, when a Detroit newspaper publicized pictures of the spotted Ocicat, that many people including cat breeders began to show a lot of interest in the new breed. Dr. Clyde Keeler, a geneticist at Georgia University, became particularly interested in the new breed, noting that it would be great to have a domestic cat with similar features as wild cats whose population was fast dwindling. It is from this point that many breeders begun developing other Ocicat breed lines and in the process exporting the breed to other regions of the world.

The Ocicat gained recognition by The International Cat Association (TICA) in 1987, a recognition that granted it Championship status. The breed has since been presented in different regional, national and international championships and has won many awards. Ocicats are now common sites in many locations across the globe.

Different cat associations around the word have also registered Ocicat kittens. Likewise, Ocicat owners and fanciers in different regions of the word have also formed specific Ocicat Clubs with the aim of furthering the development of this unique cat breed. Dedicated Ocicat clubs, breeders and associations can now be found across all states in America and other regions including Africa, Europe, South America, Canada and Asia.

Myths Associated with Ocicats

There are simply many myths associated with Ocicats and cats in general. Regrettably, some of these myths have hindered some homeowners who otherwise would love to have an Ocicat as a pet.

One of the common myths that relate to the Ocicat breed is one that portrays the breed as one susceptible to myriad of diseases and hereditary health conditions, which makes the breed a costly one to maintain. Nothing can be further from the truth. Since the first cross-breeding between an Abyssinian and a Siamese, the

Ocicat breed has undergone a lot of improvement aimed at making it less susceptible to both acquired and hereditary diseases and health conditions. Indeed, Ocicats have minimal health problems compared to other cat breeds.

The other misleading myth relating to the Ocicat relates to its appearance. Looking at an adult Ocicat is similar to looking at a dwarfed leopard. The myth that the cat at times exhibits wild behaviours and temperament is completely false. Like the Abyssinian breed, the Ocicat breed is human oriented. Not only is the breed very friendly but also thrives in the presence of humans. Ocicats feel very lonely when left on their own without any human around.

Because of their wild appearance, some have come to believe that Ocicats jump all over and never get injured since they land on their feet. While it is true that the Ocicat is playful, just in the same way as the Abyssinian from whom it was bred from, it is not a pet that jumps all over. Furthermore, Ocicats are susceptible to injuries when they jump from high heights, just like other cat breeds. In any case, although all cats land on their feet when jumping from high places, the chances that they can get injured remain real.

Pros and Cons of Owning an Ocicat

Pros

The Ocicat's biggest asset that makes it the cat of choice for many homeowners is its appearance. It's dotts or spots give it a leopard-like appearance that turns out to be very attractive. It is indeed the most attractive cat that a homeowner can have.

Like with the Abyssinian breed, the Ocicat breed is playful and prefers to be in the company of family members. It therefore makes a very good companion. The breed adores humans.

Unlike some cats, Ocicats adapt very easily to new environments. Not only will an Ocicat remain friendly and confident in a new home; it will get along extremely well with children and other pets including dogs and chickens.

The Ocicat is a very intelligent and inquisitive cat. This makes it one of the cat breeds that is very easy to train. Many Ocicat breeders indeed present the view that training Ocicats is much easier than training other cat breeds.

Cons

Unlike the Abyssinian cat, which is predominantly an indoor cat, the Ocicat is both an indoor and outdoor cat. It cannot only venture outdoors but roam widely.

The Ocicat borrows heavily from one of its breeder-parent, the Abyssinian. For instance, it is just as playful as the Abyssinian. Although this makes it a very good companion cat, the same exposes it to risk of injuries.

Chapter 3 – Psychology Of the Ocicat

The psychology of the Ocicat refers to the breed's mental functions and behaviour. The fact that it is a relatively new breed obtained through cross-breeding between an Abyssinian, a Siamese and an American Shorthair makes its behaviour very predictable. This is so because it exhibits traits of all the three distinct cat breeds.

Even so, it is still very important that you acquaint yourself with its specific traits to help you understand your Ocicat in order to live with it in the best way possible. The best way to understand the Ocicat's psychology is to first understand the three other breeds.

Believed to have originated from Ethiopia, the Abyssinian breed is one of the oldest cat breeds. It is a slender, medium-sized cat whose major characteristic is its ticked coat. With a wedge-shaped head, the Abyssinian is one of the very popular cats preferred by many homeowners around the world, mainly because of its high intelligence and the fact that it is people-oriented. It is a playful cat with a willful personality. Shy of strangers, the Abyssinian cat is predominantly an indoor cat, although it occasionally ventures outdoors.

The Siamese is an Oriental cat native to Thailand. It has a triangular-shaped head with almond-shaped eyes. It features a slender, elongated and muscular body with distinct markings. It is a very affectionate and intelligent cat that is highly social. It can be very vocal with a low-pitched and loud voice. Unlike most cat breeds, the Siamese is not active at night because of its poor night vision.

Although the American Shorthair cat breed has its origin in America, the cat was developed from several domestic shorthair cat breeds brought into America by American settlers travelling back to America from Europe. The breeding program put in place in the 19th century yielded the American Shorthair, one of the most powerful cat breeds in existence. The cat has a solidly-built body that is muscular with a well-developed chest, shoulders and hindquarters.

American Shorthair   Siamese

The Abyssinian   Ocicat

Ocicat Aggression

An offspring of three distinct breeds, the Ocicat presents a larger-than-life personality coupled with enhanced confidence. It is an outgoing cat that develops a very strong bond with family members and in particular with its master. Although very friendly to family members and strangers alike, it is bound to show some form of aggression, especially when stressed and in a hostile environment, in which case it can present either an offensive or defensive aggression.

You are most likely to observe offensive aggression if you have a male Ocicat who is not neutered. Unlike defensive aggression, offensive aggression is not triggered by anything; your Ocicat simply becomes aggressive with the intention of intimidating or bullying a fellow Ocicat, a different pet or when it wants to be alone.

Your Ocicat will exhibit several signs when in offensive aggression mode including ears facing forward when walking toward a target, constricted pupils, serious focus on target, crouching down in readiness to pounce on target and stiff tail before attack.

It is very normal to observe offensive aggression between two male Ocicats if you have two or several of them. Like all cats, the dominant male among your cats will want to stamp its authority and create clear levels of hierarchy within their territory, something it will accomplish through offensive aggression.

On the other hand, you are most likely to observe defensive aggression in your Ocicat when it is in danger or under threat. This is a way of self defense and it will do so with its ears in a flat position facing the tail, wide open eyes, arched back, curved tail, raised fur, open mouth with teeth open and walking sideways toward the enemy while hissing.

There are several causes of aggression in cats depending on the environment and situation. Of all causes, eye contact is probably the main cause. Cats generally perceive direct eye contact as a threat to them and are therefore bound to defend themselves even when not provoked.

Your Ocicat will also show signs of aggression when in pain and particularly after a traumatic experience. Something unique about cat aggression is their tendency to re-direct their aggression to something else or to you. Your Ocicat can therefore re-direct its aggression toward a stranger by lurching toward you as a way of letting out the aggression.

There are several ways through which you can deal with your Ocicat's aggression. Neutering has the positive effect of mellowing a cat's aggressive tendency and is highly recommended.

Some cat owners whose cats become too aggressive to a point of engaging in regular fights with other cats or pets at home tie a small bell on the collar to warn other cats or pets of the coming of the aggressive cat, giving the others opportunity to move away. The other alternative is to remove what causes aggression in your Ocicat, even if it means restricting it to a specific room or space in the house.

Unlike most cat breeds, the Ocicat breed is very fond of children and will only show signs of aggression when mishandled. It is therefore very important to educate your kids on how to handle the Ocicat in the course of play. Like other cat breeds, however, your Ocicat will want to remain in its comfort zone.

Your kids can push it to the extreme to a point where it turns aggressive. It becomes necessary therefore to monitor and supervise when kids play with your Ocicat. It is important to note that your Ocicat's aggression may not necessarily be a behavioural sign. It can be because of a medical problem, which makes it necessary to consult a veterinarian for assessment.

Intelligence

Intelligence here refers to your Ocicat's capacity to solve problems, learn and adapt to its surroundings. From the onset, Ocicats adapt to new environments very easily so long as they are well treated and provided for. Ocicat kittens in particular get used to new environments very fast because they set out to explore any new environment they are introduced to.

Ocicats also have a very good memory, which contributes to their high level of intelligence. The play activities your Ocicat engages in do not only serve as its way of life or behavior, it learns a lot from such activities and it is only appropriate that you have many but different cat toys.

Play activities help them in exercising their minds and in honing their natural skills. However, your Ocicat's memory will diminish once old-age sets in, coupled with the occurrence of old age-related diseases and health conditions. Because of its good memory and high level of intelligence, the Ocicat breed is the easiest cat to train. You can train your Ocicat to do almost anything in the house as long as this does not pose any risk.

Curiosity

You should not be surprised by your Ocicat's high level of curiosity. This is a trait it borrows from one of its original parents, the Abyssinian. Ocicats are naturally curious cats that always want to know what is happening in their environment. In addition to exploring their immediate surroundings, Ocicats will always try to venture outdoors.

Rubbing

Like cats in the wild, your Ocicat has the natural instinct of marking its territory and everything else within that territory. You will observe your Ocicat rubbing itself on your legs, on furniture and on the walls. This is a natural behaviour that should not be of serious concern. While rubbing itself against everything in sight, your Ocicat releases pheromones through its scent glands located on its tail and other parts of the body. You have the option of neutering/spaying your Ocicat in case this behaviour is extreme.

Kneading

Kneading is a natural behaviour of all cats regardless of breed. You will observe your Ocicat, when in a relaxed position on the couch, push out one of its front paws before pulling it back again and doing the same with the other paw, catching on clothing in the process. This is a natural behaviour that comes first before a cat falls into sleep.

Body Language

Of all your Ocicat's signs and signals, the signs and signals it sends out through its body language are very important. Your Ocicat's body posture at any given time serves as an indication of its state of mind. Your Ocicat will behave in a particular manner when it is in a relaxed position. Whether lying down or sitting, it will most likely have its legs bent, the tail loosely wrapped and extended. These will be accompanied by normal breathing.

There are times when your Ocicat will exhibit alert body posture, in which case it will lie down on its belly with its back horizontal. Although its breathing may be normal, it will have its legs either bent or extended with the tail curved toward the back. It may twitch its tail from one side to another. This is usually the behaviour of a cat focused on something such as a live prey.

Tensed cats usually present body posture in such a way that the back remains lower than its upper body while lying down. Your Ocicat may be moving forward or backwards with its hind legs bent and the front legs extended. The tail may be curled downwards or curled up. This is usually a clear sign of aggression.

Your Ocicat and a female one in particular will once in a while present a body posture where the back of its body is the only part of the body that remains visible with the front part less visible. This can happen when it is lying down on its belly or when in a standing position. The breathing in most cases is usually fast with the tail very close to the body in a curled position. This is usually a sign of anxiety. It can also be a sign that your female Ocicat is on heat if it is not spayed.

You should find it easy to know when your Ocicat is fearful. It will most likely be in a crouched position on its paws with its entire body shaking. The tail will remain close to its body and curled. It will probably try to increase its size.

19

Your Ocicat cat will not only serve you as a pet and a companion; it will also serve to warn you of possible dangers within the house or compound. Any body language sign or signal your Ocicat sends out needs immediate attention since it may notice a threat long before you do.

Vocals

Your Ocicat will on different occasions meow in different ways that communicate different things. There are times when your Ocicat will purr, which is usually a sign that it is content. It is however important to note that your Ocicat can also purr as one way of comforting itself, especially when in pain.

As a companion, the Ocicat cat is highly responsible. Your Ocicat will naturally develop the habit of welcoming you whenever you come in through the door before rubbing itself against your legs as a show of affection. It will usually do this while meowing in a soft and low tone. This can be accompanied with purring.

Loud, high-pitched, frantic and repeated meowing is usually a sign of danger or distress. You will need to respond to such calls immediately since your Ocicat will be in dire need of help.

Your Ocicat is an attention seeking cat and will do everything it can to have your attention. It will seek your attention through simple meows, which can be loud and high-pitched when your attention is not forthcoming.

Panting

Although cats generally do not pant like dogs, there are times when your Ocicat will pant. This will most likely be when travelling in a car, when stressed, when anxious and when on heat among other situations. You will however take note of excessive panting as a sign of illness.

House Soiling

House soiling is the most disturbing behaviour you will most likely observe your Ocicat engage in. House soiling simply means urinating or defecating all over instead of using a provided litter box.

While it is perfectly normal for your Ocicat to urinate (spray) outside its litter box, defecating outside the litter box can be because of other reasons. Your Ocicat will most likely spray outside its litter box as one way of marking its territory. Unlike regular urination, your Ocicat will spray while standing and probably with one leg raised instead of squatting. Spraying becomes common when you have several cats in the house, in which case the dominant cat (usually a male) marks its territory.

Urination and defecation outside the litter box can be because of several reasons, one of which is a medical problem. Any inflammation of your Ocicat's urinary tract will cause frequent and sometimes painful urination. Because it is most likely to associate the pain it experiences with the litter box, it will avoid it. The other reason may be because of the urgency to urinate when the litter box is in a different room.

Another reason for house soiling can simply be aversion. Your Ocicat may find the litter box unsuitable for several reasons including bad odour, high-sided litter box, dirty litter box, distasteful litter box and inappropriate location of the litter box.

House soiling can be very traumatizing. It is therefore very important that you take all necessary measures to find out why your Ocicat engages in this form of behaviour. It is always recommended that you take your Ocicat to a vet for assessment in case there is no apparent reason for house soiling.

Confusion

Your Ocicat may suddenly become confused, in which case it is most likely to get lost in very familiar locations, stare into space, wander aimlessly and forget where its room is located. Confusion in cats is normally accompanied by partial disorientation. Although this is usually a sign of old age setting in, it can also be a sign of illness, which requires attention from your vet.

Poor Social Behaviour

Ocicats are generally highly social animals and very friendly. Your Ocicat will not be in the habit of avoiding play or welcoming you when you come into the house. You may however observe your Ocicat withdrawing to be alone or simply seek too much attention by becoming over-independent on you. Although this is a sign of old age, it can also be a sign of illness.

Chapter 4 – Appearance Of The Ocicat

General Appearance

Keeping an Ocicat is like keeping a dwarf leopard at home. This is so because the cat presents a wild Leopard-like appearance. Its facial features, its movement and spotted sleek coat indeed transform the otherwise domestic cat into a wild creature. The cat is not only athletic in appearance but is also large. It is solidly built with short but strong bones. The spots on the coat look like thumbprints. It has a tight coat with markings evenly distributed on the body.

Head

The Ocicat features a wedged head with a slight curve running from its muzzle to the cheek. The area between the bridge and brow rises gently. Its bridge is very pronounced as it is not only somehow lengthy but also appears squared. The cat has firm jaws coupled with a strong chin.

Ocicat ears are characteristically large and in an alert position most of the time. The ears are well positioned on the upper part of either side of the head. The cat has large, almond-shaped eyes that angle upwards toward the ears, giving it the wild facial appearance.

Body

The Ocicat has a large body that is not only long but also full. It exhibits substantial bone development yet presents an athletic appearance. Although the body remains level, it tends to rise slightly towards the rear. The cat's legs are characteristically well muscled and look powerful. It has a long tail that tapers slightly towards the tip.

Coat

The Ocicat features a short and smooth coat with a lustrous sheen. The coat is low-lying and long to perfectly accommodate bands of colour. The coat has a distinct pattern that is clearly visible on the forehead where an intricate "M" pattern forms, running from the forehead to the area between the ears before extending down towards the neck and shoulder regions where the pattern breaks into tiny spots. Other areas of the cat's coat with distinct markings include both the eyes and cheek areas that have Mascara markings, the spine that features rows of spots that run from shoulder blades towards the tail and a broken necklace at the throat.

Colour

Of all cat breeds, the Ocicat is the most colourful cat you can find. Each hair on its coat contains not one but several colours. Although there are six recognized championship colours, you are most likely to find an Ocicat in a different colour that is not recognized.

Recognized championship colours include Tawny (black or brown spotting), Chocolate (chocolate spotting), Cinnamon (bright cinnamon spotting), Blue (blue spotting), Lilac (lilac spotting) and Fawn (fawn spotting). You are also likely to find a Black silver, chocolate silver, Cinnamon silver, blue silver, Lilac silver, fawn silver, Lavender spotted and Ebony silver-coloured Ocicats.

Body Weight

Ocicats are generally large cats with well developed bones. They not only look powerful but are indeed powerful. Athletic and sleek, an adult mature male Ocicat weighs between 9 pounds and 14 pounds (between 4 kg and 6 kg). Females weigh less, between 6 pounds and 9 pounds (between 3 kg and 4 kg).

Temperament

The Ocicat is probably the loveliest cat you can have at home as a pet. Not only is it very friendly to family members but to strangers as well. It is a very active cat that rarely stays idle, unless it is sick. The fact that it gets along perfectly well with other pets such as dogs makes it the best cat you can have. An un-neutered male Ocicat will however tend to be dominant over all other pets at home, which may be a cause of trouble. Being people oriented, the Ocicat is an attention-seeking cat that goes to great lengths to get your attention.

Chapter 5 – Buying An Ocicat

Although a relatively new breed of cat, the Ocicat breed is fast becoming popular across the world. There are several ways through which you can obtain an Ocicat to keep as a pet:

From Your Neighbor or a Friend

This is the easiest way to acquire an Ocicat. You can have a neighbour with Ocicat kittens, in which case you may buy or simply receive one or several for free. This way of acquiring an Ocicat or any other pet for that matter is not recommended for several reasons. Firstly, the kitten you buy may not necessarily be pure bred. Secondly, you may acquire kittens with serious health problems.

From a Rescue Center

You are likely to find either a general cat rescue center or a dedicated Ocicat rescue center depending on your location. While some of these centers offer rescued Ocicats for adoption, others sell them off to obtain necessary funds for maintaining other rescued pets. Gaining possession of an Ocicat from a rescue center may not be appropriate because caretakers are not necessarily knowledgeable about them. This simply means that you will not receive the necessary advice on how to maintain your cat in the most recommended way.

Pet Store

There are dedicated pet stores that offer Ocicats for sale. While some of such stores are breeder outlets, others are operated by individual owners who may not have sufficient information regarding the breed.

From a Breeder

The increasing popularity of the Ocicat breed across the world has made it possible for the establishment of many catteries to cater for the increasing demand for this cat. Some of the established catteries have a very long history, having been in the business of breeding other cat breeds.

Well established breeders around the world are members of different organization and associations. Such organizations/associations include The International Cat Association (TICA), Ocicat Club (UK), Ocicats of North America Club, OCIcat (Finland) and American Cat Fanciers Association (CFA). Different Ocicat owners in specific regions and locations in the world have also formed Ocicat clubs for the purpose of sharing information about the breed.

Buying an Ocicat from an Ocicat breeder provides for several benefits. Although buying from a breeder can be expensive depending on your location, the quality of a cat you buy is no doubt high. This is because breeders put in a lot of effort in ensuring that a kitten or cat you buy is not only properly vaccinated but is also free of common Ocicat health problems.

How to Choose a Breeder
Although buying an Ocicat from a breeder is highly recommended, it is very important that you choose an Ocicat breeder carefully. Doing so makes it possible for you to buy a healthy cat.

One of the things you need to look into is whether or not a breeder is a member of a regional or a national association. Such breeders do adhere to codes of ethics formulated by associations. A reputable breeder should be available for consultation when it becomes necessary long after purchasing your cat.

It is also very important that you ascertain whether or not an Ocicat breeder you plan to buy from has all the requisite certifications and, in particular, certifications relating to screening out of genetic health problems.

Perhaps a good way to choose the right breeder lies in consulting with your local veterinarian, who is in a better position to know local Ocicat breeders.

Questions to Ask

There are a number of critical questions that you need to ask an Ocicat breeder before you make any financial commitments. A reputable breeder should not only answer your questions; he/she should be prepared to answer them in detail. Asking some or all of the questions relating to the following will be of great benefit to you.

Experience

You need to choose an Ocicat breeder with some years of experience in breeding cats and in particular Ocicats. It is also important to ascertain whether or not a breeder participates in cat shows. Breeders who participate in cat shows do not only have the experience but valuable knowledge as well, knowledge that will benefit you as the breeder will certainly share it with you.

Breeding Style

It is very important that you ascertain a breeder's breeding style before you buy. A knowledgeable breeder will normally adopt a breeding style that addresses Ocicat health problems. Buying from such a breeder ensures that you will buy a cat with very minimal health issues to deal with.

Vaccinations

Like with all other animals, it is good to know if a breeder's Ocicats receive the requisite vaccinations before they are sold off. It is very important that you only buy vaccinated cats because they will be your indoor pets.

Guarantees

Although not offered by all Ocicat breeders, buying a cat with a health guarantee can be very beneficial to you. A cat that you buy

can fall ill within days of buying and it is only appropriate that
you have some level of guarantee.

Certification
In addition to a breeder's certification, it is good to ascertain
whether or not parents of a cat you are about to buy are certified.
This simply means that a cat whose parents are certified will not
be at risk of suffering genetic health conditions.

These are just a few of the many critical questions that you need
to ask an Ocicat breeder. Doing so will make it possible for you to
buy a quality cat that is easy to maintain in terms of veterinary
costs. You may, however, need to realize that finding a specialized
Ocicat breeder may be a problem because it is a relatively new
breed. Most breeders who offer Ocicat kittens for sale are general
breeders who breed other cat breeds.

How to Choose a Healthy Ocicat
The Ocicat breed is fast becoming the favourite cat breed for
homeowners looking for cats to keep as pets. This can be partly
attributed to the fact that the Ocicat breed is an improved version
of the Abyssinian breed, the other popular breed with a long
history. Note that the Ocicat breed was obtained by cross-
breeding three distinct breeds, one of which is the Abyssinian.

Whether buying an adult Ocicat or kitten, identifying a healthy
one to buy should not be a problem. One way to go about doing
so lies in asking a breeder to see a kitten's parents. The fact that
Ocicats are active cats makes it necessary that you pay attention
to its parents' level of activity. A kitten or cat you are planning to
buy should also be active.

Your first impression of a cat or kitten you are interested in is also
important. Watch out for the cat's behaviour towards you.
Generally, Ocicats are receptive and may try out some form of
play with you. Examine the eyes, ears, nose, mouth, anal area,

weight and temperament. Ascertain whether a cat you are interested in buying has any discharges in the mentioned areas.

Undertaking a pre-purchase examination is also very important. A reputable Ocicat breeder will normally allow you to visit with a qualified veterinarian for such examination. A vet should be in a position to perform a number of routine tests including the cat's general blood work, viral tests, stool/urine analysis and a general physical examination.

Ocicats are generally affordable, although they can also be expensive depending on a breeder and your location. This makes it necessary to have a purchase agreement. Reputable breeders do have agreements prepared. Even so, it is important that you pay attention to agreement provisions and in particular sections that address your responsibilities.

Pure Bred or Crossbred and Why

This is one of the most important decisions you have to make when planning to buy a cat. Like with other cat breeds, you will come across purebred and crossbred Ocicats.

Buying a purebred Ocicat can be beneficial to you, considering that you end up with a cat whose personality and characteristics you know perfectly well. Furthermore, buying a purebred cat makes it possible for you to deal with known health challenges that the Ocicat breed is susceptible to. Although crossbred Ocicats do face similar health challenges as purebred Ocicats, theirs may be complicated to deal with because of genetic alterations. The cost of purebred Ocicats is usually higher than that of crossbreds.

Where to Buy

Unlike most cat breeds, the Ocicat breed is relatively new. It is because of this that there are only a few specialized Ocicat breeders around the world. The few specialized breeders are mostly to be found in the USA, Australia and in some European countries. The majority of Ocicat breeders are therefore general breeders who are also involved in breeding other cat breeds.

Ocicat prices vary a great deal depending on several factors. Factors such as breeder, location, quality of breed and services offered come into play when determining the Ocicat price. The following are just a few breeders who breed Ocicats. It is important to check out the breeders. I have obviously not visited all these breeders so I cannot speak from personal experience from any of the breeders listed below. However, I've checked on forums and people who have bought from these breeders are happy with their purchase.

Marafiki (http://www.marafiki.co.uk)

Marafiki is a family-owned cattery based in Worthing in South-East England. This is one of the catteries whose owners were first Abyssinia cat owners before turning breeders. The cattery now breeds Ocicats.

Marafiki is a Kiswahili language term that literally translates to "friends", something attributable to both the Ocicat and Abyssinian breeds. The cattery participates in various cat shows where Marafiki Ocicats and Abyssinians have always been admired.

Calumet Cats Ocicats (www.calumetcats.com)

Named after the famous Calumet Farms in Michigan, USA, Calumet Cats Ocicats is one of the few specialized Ocicat breeders not only in the USA but also in the world. The breeder has gained the reputation of breeding healthy Ocicats mainly for competitions and actively participates in cat shows in Michigan, Indiana, Ohio and in Canada. The breeder also sells Ocicat kittens and adults.

Midnite Moon Ocicat (www.midnitemoonocicats.com)

Located in Ohio in the USA, this is another specialized Ocicat breeder who started as a cat owner. The cattery is registered by both TICA and CFA. What started off as a family owning an Ocicat has today turned into a major cattery that has become to be known for breeding high quality Ocicats that have won several championship awards, including the prestigious CFA's Grand Premier Title.

Purrfurdots Ocicats (www.purrfurdotsocicats.com)

This is one of the notable specialized Ocicat breeders in the USA. Located in Gettysburg, Pennsylvania, this is one breeder who breeds both pure bred and A.O.V. (any other variety) CFA registered Ocicat kittens throughout the year. However, you may need to book in advance since the breeder's kittens are always high in demand. You are obligated to pay a deposit of $100 when you book.

Unlike most Ocicat breeders, this is one of the most affordable breeders you can find in Pennsylvania. The breeder is also one amongst many who sells Ocicat kittens with a one-year guarantee. While pure bred spotted Ocicat kittens sell at $500, A.O.Vs sell at $400. Apart from various Championship awards, the breeder's kittens and cats have received prizes in various Ocicat shows and championships, and the breeder has continuously received the coveted "CFA Cattery of Excellence" award for maintaining high standards of breeding Ocicats.

JumpnSpots (www.jumpnspotsocicats.com)

This breeder is located a few hours drive towards the north of Los Angeles along the road to Santa Barbara. The breeders are two sisters (Zoe and Stella) who specialize in breeding pure bred spotted Ocicats. With breeding experience spanning ten years, the sisters have now incorporated the Savannah breed into their cattery.

The cattery's kittens do turn out to be highly social. This is because, apart from the family's children who interact with both the cats and kittens regularly, the family also keeps German dogs that engage the cats in play activities. Both the breeder's Ocicats and Savannah cats are pure breeds registered with both TICA and CFA.

Aalspotz (www.aalspotz.co.uk)

This can be said to be one of the most successful breeders in the UK. Owned by Paul and Sue Threapleton, the cattery is located in a village in the East Yorkshire area. In a locality full of animals, the family started off breeding and exhibiting Fancy Rats and Mice that became very popular with Fancy Rat show goers in the late 1999s and early 2006.

The family eventually abandoned breeding Fancy Rats and Mice in favour of dogs and rabbits. Although they had cats, they were just pets. It was not long before the family resorted to breeding cats with the intention of breeding one of the relatively new cat breeds. Although the family wanted to breed the Egyptian Mau, they settled on the Ocicat breed for its beautiful appearance. The family now focuses on breeding Ocicats with special focus on reproducing kittens with good health, good temperament and great looks.

Manchado (www.manchado.co.uk)

This is a professional breeder of both Savannah and Ocicats. Located in Chilterns (UK), the breeder is registered by both TICA as a Savannah cat breeder and by GCCF as an Ocicat breeder. The breeder sells both Ocicat and Savannah kittens when they attain the age of 12 weeks. This is to give the mothers enough time to wean them in addition to educating them on valuable lessons, including how to use a litter tray. All kittens sold by the breeder are sold with a pedigree certificate and insurance cover.

Vervain (www.vervain.co.uk)

Vervain cats are very popular in the UK. This breeder is located in Nottinghamshire and is registered by GCCF, FIFE and TICA as a breeder of Ocicats, Asian and Burmese cats. The cattery is owned by Naomi Johnson, whose cats have won several awards in cat shows and championships including the Grand Champion and the UK Premier Vervain Goldberry Awards.

Ocivic (www.ocivic.com)

This is a small, home-based breeder located in Melbourne, Australia. The breeder sells Ocicat kittens when they have already been vaccinated, complete with pedigree certificates. The breeder has over the past few years managed to sell cats to other states in Australia.

KezKatz (www.kezkatz.com)

Located in Oklahoma, USA, KezKatz is a breeder of Ocicats, Egyptian Maus and Savannah cats. The cattery is registered by both TICA and CFA as a specialized breeder of exotic cat breeds. This is one of a few breeders in the USA licensed to export and import cats. The cattery now exports cats including Ocicats to different regions of the world.

Ameeka (www.ameeka.co.uk)

This is one of the Ocicat breeders in the UK. The cattery is located on the outkirts of Lincoln City. In addition to Ocicats, the breeder is also in the business of breeding Abyssinans and Ocicat Classics.

Anizz (www.anizz.co.uk)

This cattery is located in Rugby, Warwickshire in the UK. Owned by Mr./Mrs Robert Anita, it is one of the few catteries in the UK that has ventured into breeding Ocicats. They also breed Classic Ocicats and Tiffanies. The couple had been used to keeping cats and dogs long before they ventured into the breeding of cats. Their encounter with the Ocicat breed at a cat show made them change from being cat owners to cat breeders with special attention on the Ocicat breed.

Thickthorn Ocicats (www.ocicats.org.uk)

This is a specialized Ocicat breeder located within Hampshire in the UK. The breeder has a big cattery that is not only cat oriented but also properly equipped to cater for the interests of Ocicats. This is one of a few catteries that breeds both male and female Ocicats with a dedicated area reserved for males. Most kittens sold by this breeder are usually neutered or spayed.

Wild Thing (www.wildthingcats.com.cu)

This is the first cat breeder to have introduced the Ocicat into Australia. Although the breeder concentrated on breeding other cat breeds in the past, the Ocicat is now the main focus. The breeder aims at breeding enough Ocicat kittens to satisfy the increasing demand for the Ocicat breed in Australia. It must be noted that very few homeowners and cat lovers in Australia have had the opportunity to buy Ocicats.

Zayenah (www.zayenahocicats.com)

This is one of a few specialized Ocicat breeders in Australia. The cattery is located in Adelaide in South Australia. The breeder is registered by both Feline Association of South Australia (FASA) and the Governing Council of the Cat Fancy of South Australia (GCCFSA). Apart from breeding, the breeder is also a recognized Ocicat show participant. The breeder's cats have indeed won several cat show awards in Australia including both the 2009 and 2011 GCCFSA Ocicat of the Year Award.

What age to buy and why

Although you have the option of buying an adult Ocicat or kitten, there are several factors you need to consider before buying. One of these factors has to do with age of your children and in particular children aged below six years. This is in case you have children at home. Although Ocicats are generally fond of children, having young children at home may make it necessary for you to buy an Ocicat aged two years and above. This will be a cat capable of understanding children.

Being a senior citizen makes it necessary to avoid buying Ocicat kittens at all costs. This is because kittens can be very mischievous and troublesome. They need constant watch, a task you may not be comfortable performing. You may therefore need to buy an Ocicat aged at least two years. Note that buying a much older cat may not be appropriate considering that Ocicats have a general lifespan of 15 years.

How much time you plan to spend with your cat is also a very important factor to consider. Buy an Ocicat aged at least three years if you will not be at home all the time, unless you plan to have someone at home on a regular basis.

You may consider buying an Ocicat kitten if you take into consideration the element of training. Ocicat breeders do offer kittens aged at least 12 weeks for sale. Although a kitten you buy will have received some level of basic training, you will still have the opportunity to offer the kind of training to suit your home and your preferences.

One challenge that you may face when you buy a kitten is in determining its personality. The fact that you are not in a position to determine a kitten's personality at such a young age may make it necessary to buy a mature Ocicat.

One or more and why

The decision on whether to buy one, two or more Ocicats depends on several factors, one of which is resources. You may opt to buy two cats if you are financially capable of meeting their feeding, care, grooming and health needs. You also need to consider the amount of space you have in your house. Although you may be comfortable with only one, it would be ideal if you buy two for their own company.

Male or Female and why

Different people have different preferences when it comes to the gender of a pet they plan to buy and the same applies to buying Ocicats. While there are those who prefer male cats, there are also those comfortable with female cats.

The most important thing to note is that whether you choose to buy a male or a female Ocicat, each gender has its pros and cons. Like with other male cats of other breeds, a male Ocicat will roam in search of a female to mate with. Male Ocicats also tend to mark their territory both indoors and outdoors, which creates an environment where cat fights may be the order of the day when you introduce another male cat or a different pet or in case there is another in your neighbourhood.

Likewise, a female Ocicat will also roam in search of a mating partner when on heat. Note that a female Ocicat, like with other female cat breeds, will come on heat regularly until such a time when it finds a mate, a period that can last up to 16 days. Female

Ocicats usually become sexually mature once they attain the age of six months and you may not find it comfortable living with a female Ocicat on heat considering that she will keep on calling day and night.

Such problems should not in any way deter you from owning either gender of the Ocicat. You can have your kitten or adult cat de-sexed before you bring him/her home. De-sexing is the procedure where cats and other animals are subjected to surgical routines that make them incapable of reproducing. De-sexing literally kills their sex drive. While de-sexing in male animals is professionally known as neutering, it is spaying for female animals.

Neutering/Spaying

Neutering in male animals including Ocicat males involves the removal of the testes. This renders your cat sterile, which provides for several benefits. On the other hand, spaying in female animals including Ocicat females involves the removal of the ovaries and uterus. There are cases where only the ovaries are removed. Like with neutering, spaying also provides for several benefits.

Advantages of Neutering/Spaying

Having your cat neutered or spayed can be beneficial to you in many ways. In addition to being a birth control method, neutering/spaying transforms your cat's general behaviour. A male Ocicat that has been neutered will not only show reduced aggression tendencies; it will also change its mounting and urine spaying behaviour. Likewise, a female Ocicat that has been spayed will show less aggression towards males due to the reduction in levels of sex hormones.

One of the biggest advantages of having your Ocicat neutered/spayed is in the elimination of roaming. Female cats do produce pheromones into the air when they are on heat. Pheromones are chemical signals that attract male cats for mating.

A neutered cat does not react on sensing pheromones in the air and will therefore not roam in search for the cat on heat. On the other hand, a spayed female cat is incapable of releasing pheromones and will therefore not roam in search of a male.

The benefits of having your cat de-sexed are not restricted to behavioural changes. There are health benefits as well. Spaying a female Ocicat relieves it of anxiety and stress she would otherwise have when on heat and denied the opportunity to mate. Note that a female cat on heat can remain in the same state for up to 16 days and is bound to be stressed without an opportunity to mate. The female's condition is even made worse by the fact that it is bound to come on heat again after about 14 days after the initial phase.

Like with other cat breeds, female Ocicats are susceptible to mammary cancer, which is mainly caused by reproduction hormones. Spaying reduces the risk of mammary cancer by between 30 and 50%. Spaying also reduces the risk of such health problems as reproduction tract tumours and other associated infections.

Another benefit that de-sexing your cat provides relates to the amount of money you would incur in maintenance. The cost of maintaining a de-sexed cat is relatively lower compared to maintaining a cat that has not been subjected to the same.

When to Have Your Cat Neutered/Spayed

There is really no fixed age at which you can have your cat neutered or spayed. You only need to consult with your veterinarian to perform the necessary surgical operation. A trend that is now emerging is where breeders offer for sale neutered/spayed kittens and cats before selling them off, saving you from the cost and the trouble of looking for a veterinarian to perform the procedure.

Ocicat breeders in the USA in particular neuter male kittens when they are about four months old. Some breeders neuter them when they are only six weeks old. Likewise, females are spayed when they are between 5 and 8 years old. Some breeders spay them when they are only 2 months of age. Contrary to a common belief, neutering/spaying kittens at such a tender age does not hinder their overall development. Neutering/spaying kittens is also beneficial since they have the opportunity to heal faster than when de-sexing is performed when they are mature. Apart from breeders, you can have your cat neutered/spayed by your local veterinarian.

Chapter 6 – How to Prepare For Your Ocicat

What to Know Before You Buy

There are a number of things you need to know before you buy a pet or an Ocicat for that matter. Knowing some of these things will make living with your cat not only easy but an enjoyable experience as well.

Buying an Ocicat is similar to introducing a new member into your family. You will be obligated to treat your cat in the same way that you do to your family members. You therefore need to be prepared to cater for your cat's needs in terms of food, veterinary care, shelter, grooming and love.

Buying a cat is a life-long commitment. You need to be prepared to live with your cat for long. Note that although Ocicats have a general life span of about 15 years, they can actually live much longer depending on the quality of life you subject them to.

Like the Abyssinian, the Ocicat breed is an attention-seeker. You will need to spend a considerable amount of time with your cat. Furthermore, be prepared to be watched keenly. This is because in addition to seeking your attention, your Ocicat will watch everything that you do and do not be surprised if what you thought you had hidden is eventually retrieved.

The Ocicat breed is both an indoor and outdoor pet. Although it spends most of the time indoors, it occasionally ventures outdoors not only to play but to explore as well. It is therefore very important that both the indoor and outdoor environments are pet friendly.

Bring your cat home only when everything is in place. Do not bring the cat home before you have enough food supply and other essentials such as bowls and play toys.

Scratching is an innate characteristic of all cat breeds, the Ocicat breed included. Ensure that you have a scratch post strategically located for your cat's convenience.

Although you will occasionally groom your cat, you need to note that it will also indulge in self-grooming most of the time. You will therefore need to make your cat used to a specific spot for grooming.

The most important thing you cannot ignore when you are about to bring your Ocicat home is to cat-proof your house and establish a safe room. Cat-proofing your house simply means making your house as secure as possible for the benefit of your cat. This you can do by removing or storing sharp objects that stand out. A safe room does not necessarily mean a room preserved for the cat. It simply refers to a specific location such as an ideal corner within one of the rooms that your cat will be trained to get used to as its "home".

Essential Supplies

There is serious need to prepare well long before you bring home your Ocicat kitten or cat. You will need to invest in a good number of items/equipments for the benefit of your pet. It is very important that you invest in high quality equipments that will serve you for a reasonable time. It is not mandatory that you must spend money in buying some of the equipments. There are some equipment that you can easily make at home in case you happen to be a DIY person. The following are some of the most essential items that you must have.

Cat Food

Food is the first item that must have before you bring your kitten or cat home. However, not all food stuffs will do. You need to buy specially formulated cat food that will allow your cat to grow strong and healthy. It is important to note that cats require specific dietary nutrients and it is only appropriate that you buy food stuffs that contain such nutrients.

Specially formulated commercial cat foods are readily available from pet food stores and it is recommended that you check at your local pet store outlet for this.

You will definitely find cat food in different forms. Like with dry food stuffs, dry cat foods contain limited moisture. They are in most cases sprayed with fat to make them palatable. They also contain added ingredients to replace vital nutrients destroyed during preparation.

Wet cat food stuffs are usually canned or in foil pouch form. There are also fortified vegetarian cat foods. Because cats are obligate carnivores, their vegetarian food is usually fortified with such ingredients as taurine and arachidonic acid, ingredients that cats are not in a position to synthesize from plants.

It is highly recommended that you buy dry, wet and vegan cat food stuffs to allow your cat have a complete diet. It is also highly recommended that you buy cat food from reputable stockists who stock cat food brands of good reputation.

Food & Water Dishes
You need to buy recommended cat food and water dishes. You need to choose your cat food and water dishes carefully, paying attention to colour and size. Doing so will make it possible for your cat to enjoy eating and drinking.

Litter Box & Scoops
By natural instinct, your cat will dig and bury its waste. It is therefore very necessary that you buy an appropriate litter box filled with clean litter. You have the option of buying an open or enclosed litter box. Self-cleaning litter boxes have of late hit the market, which you may also consider buying.

Cat Furniture
Although full of energy and very playful, your Ocicat will once in a while want to rest and catch a nap. Investing in a cat condo is therefore very appropriate. Alongside a condo should be a cat tree. A cat tree is very important because your cat will naturally want to scratch in order to sharpen its claws. Having a cat tree will save you from the agony of having your furniture scratched. An alternative to a cat tree is a cat scratching post in case you have limited space.

Cat Carrier
It is very important that you invest in a quality cat carrier. It becomes handy when you need to transport your cat to the vet or when travelling. A quality carrier should have enough room in which you can place a small cat condo.

Brush
Investing in a brush is important. This is because your Ocicat will occasionally shed and the brush will come in handy. You will also brush your cat to prevent the development of hairballs.

Collar
This is one of the most important things you cannot afford not to have when you bring your Ocicat or kitten home. This is because you never know when your cat will venture outdoors with the possibility of getting lost. A collar should have room for your cat's name, your name and address/contact.

Non-Essential Supplies
Although generally considered as non-essential cat supplies, some of the following items can be very important, especially when you need to have an active, healthy and intelligent Ocicat as a companion.

Ocicats are generally playful, which may make it necessary for you to invest in cat toys. Alternatively, consider using such readily available items as paper bags and cardboard when playing with your cat.

Although your cat will naturally scratch as one way of sharpening/cutting its claws, you may need to consider investing in a cat nail clipper for trimming its claws.

Feeding your cat dry, wet and vegetarian food stuffs should be enough to cleanse its teeth. You may however consider buying cat toothbrush and paste just to ensure that you cleanse its teeth well.

Licensing

Bringing an Ocicat home as a pet is similar to enlarging your family. The breed develops a closeness and unique attachment to all family members and considers itself part of the family. This is one of the reasons why you need to license your Ocicat. Licensing your cat is similar to buying insurance cover. Licensing it makes it easy for animal control officers to reach you in case your cat gets lost and is found.

The other reason why you need to license your cat relates to disease control. You give out vital information to animal control officers when you license your cat. Data captured during licensing benefits you in a great way. This is because you will be contacted in case of newly availed vaccinations. More importantly, licensing your cat makes it easy for animal officers, cat breeders and animal health authorities to have vital statistics necessary for planning.

Different countries have different legislations that relate to pets including cats. There are countries where cat owners are not obligated to buy licenses for their cats but are for dogs. There are also countries where licensing is compulsory for all pets.

Cat licensing requirements and fees differ across the Unites States of America. While it is mandatory in states such as Los Angeles for dogs to be licensed, licensing is not required for cats.

Likewise, there are states where it is mandatory for cats to be licensed. In addition to licensing, cats must carry proper identification. In such states, licensing is by a county's relevant animal authority. There are also states where veterinarians are given the responsibility to license cats. This is so because cat licenses are meant to last for the duration of vaccination. Cat owners therefore find it easy to renew their cat licenses when returning their cats for vaccination.

Cat licensing is mandatory in the UK. In addition, your cat will need to have a cat tag. Cat licensing in the UK is the responsibility of different authorities concerned with the welfare of cats and other pets. However, most licenses are issued by local authorities at the local level. Cat owners can also buy licenses or renew their cat licenses at animal care centers.

It is important that you do not view licensing your cat as just a legal requirement. View it as one of the most effective ways of protecting your cat. You also need to consider registering your Ocicat with your local Ocicat club or association if you happen to live in an area with an established cat club. This particularly applies in case you live in a jurisdiction where licensing of cats is not mandatory.

Micro-Chipping

Micro-chipping refers to the latest technology used in identifying lost animals and pets. Unlike externally attached Radio Frequency Identification tags commonly used to identify farm animals, micro-chipping involves the implantation of a small Radio Frequency Identification chip just under a pet's skin.

You can have your Ocicat micro-chipped. This is a service offered by veterinarians. You will have the chip implanted under your cat's skin at the back of its neck. This is the area with layers of connective tissue capable of holding the chip in place. Although the use of micro-chips is not yet widespread, there are jurisdictions where you are obligated to have your cat or other pet micro-chipped.

There are several benefits that you derive from having your cat micro-chipped. From the onset, it becomes easy for animal control officers and animal shelter organizations to contact you in case your cat gets lost and is found. Having your cat micro-chipped is also beneficial to you considering the fact that cat or pet registries, veterinarians and trainers use micro-chips to identify pets under their care.

Micro-chipping is very important and it is not surprising that many breeders including Ocicat breeders micro-chip their kittens/cats before selling them off. The chip contains information including your name, residence and contact information.

Introducing Your Cat to Your Home

Just in the same way that you take time to get used to a new environment, your Ocicat will take some time to get used to your home. Your cat may not behave in a way you expect during the first few days. It will certainly not eat and behave as you expect.

Like with any cat breed, the Ocicat breed is a territorial animal. This is why it is very important that you designate for it a room or space in your house. Your cat will naturally spend the first few days or weeks learning every sound and smell in its territory before venturing into other rooms. One of the most important things that your cat will learn is your body language and the tone of your voice. It is therefore very important that you take all these into account when communicating with your cat.

Your main task during the first few days should be to introduce your cat to its important tools. This is the time to introduce it to its litter box, feeding dishes, water dishes and furniture. Ocicats are generally fast learners and will follow minor instructions to the letter. This is also the right time to introduce one or two toys for play.

Introducing toys will make your cat get involved in play activities, which will go a long way in eliminating boredom. You will need to spend the first few days observing your cat with the aim of ascertaining its demands, which you will need to fulfill. The main point here is to make your cat feel as comfortable as possible. One thing you are most likely to observe is its act of hissing and growling at any new sound or movement. This is normal and should not be a concern.

Introducing Your Cat to other Pets

Bringing your cat home when you already have other pets and in particular another cat can be a serious challenge. This is so because the resident cat already considers your home its territory and will not welcome another cat very easily. Unlike other cat breeds however, the Ocicat breed is very receptive to other cats and pets. The challenge may be how to deal with the other cat or pet. To prevent such a scenario, it is always recommended that a cat you introduce should be of the opposite sex of the resident cat. Note that you will not be able to prevent cat fights even when both of them are desexed.

The easiest way to introduce your Ocicat to other cat(s) is to set them apart. You need to create a separate room or space for your new cat and let them bond naturally. Bringing in a new cat and housing them in the same room or space can be very problematic. You could even try feeding the two animals on opposite sides of the door so that they get used to each other's smell.

Introducing Your Cat to Family Members

Introducing your cat to family members and in particular to children the first time you bring it home is not recommended. Doing so can be stressful for the cat. It can actually feel very uncomfortable and take a while to get used to its new environment.

When to introduce your cat to family members depends on how fast it has gotten used to its room or space. While some cats take between two and four weeks to get accustomed and start interacting with family members, others take as little as few days.

It is recommended that you do not introduce your cat to several family members at the same time. Only one family member should venture into the cat's room or space with the aim of bonding with the cat. For easy bonding, a family member venturing into the cat's room or space should not stand but rather sit on the floor when communicating with the cat. Light touch is recommended for the cat to get used to the family member and build trust.

Ocicats are generally inquisitive and will naturally walk slowly toward a family member they are not used to. It is therefore very important that a family member who ventures into the cat's room or space for the first time keeps his/her distance and lets the cat walk towards him/her.

One rule of thumb that any new family member venturing into a cat's room or space for the first time needs to remember is to avoid picking up the cat. Ocicats are lap cats and do not like to be carried around. They, however, choose when to leap onto one's lap. Family members also need to note that there are times when the cat will want to have its peace and will show this by hiding underneath its furniture or bed. It should simply be left alone when this happens.

There are several ways through which you can introduce your Ocicat to other family members quickly. The first of these is for a family member venturing into the cat's room or space to engage the cat in play activities with the use of toys. Bringing the cat small amounts of food is also another great way for your cat to bond with other family members.

Although Ocicats get along well with other pets including dogs, it can still be a challenge to bring an Ocicat to a home with a dog as

49

another pet. It is always a good idea to keep your cat indoors in its room or space before you allow it to venture into other rooms or outdoors. Even so, it will be beneficial to keep the dog on a leash to allow the cat to explore its new surroundings. You will need to give your cat room to approach the dog on its own terms. Because your cat will naturally approach the dog to sniff it, you will need to be prepared to act when necessary, just in case the dog is not welcoming.

The first few days or weeks upon bringing your cat home will be very involving and challenging. It is therefore very important that you create enough time to be at home most of the time to ensure that your cat remains comfortable. The challenge eventually wears off once the cat gets used to its new environment, family members and other pets in the home.

Mistakes to Avoid

There are several serious mistakes that most new cat owners do that you need to avoid at all costs. Avoiding these mistakes goes a long way in helping your cat get used to its new environment fast enough.

One of the serious mistakes you need to avoid is to fail to make your home pet-friendly. You need to make your home pet-friendly by ensuring that all that your cat will need is in place before you bring it home. Create a special room or space. You also need to equip the room or space with all that the cat will need. These include litter box, cat furniture and food/water dishes among other vital equipments.

Ocicats are people-oriented cats and one of the costly mistakes you need to avoid is to leave your cat alone for a lengthy period of time. Leaving your cat alone for a long time can easily drive it into developing a feeling of loneliness, increased anxiety and undesired behaviours. Make it a point to have someone at home most of the time as your cat will need companionship.

Ocicats are clever and highly intelligent cats. They are very receptive to training, which you need to embark on as early as possible. Although certain training aspects will definitely require a professional trainer, teaching your Ocicat obedience commands should not be a problem. Ensure that your cat can positively respond to such minor commands as sit, stay and leave. A cat that follows commands will rarely develop untoward behaviour.

Every home has rules that family members are obligated to stick to and your home is no exception. As part of your family, do not fail to make your cat aware of simple rules, particularly when it comes to feeding time. It cannot only be embarrassing but injurious for your cat to pounce on your hands when presenting it with food. You need to avoid such behaviour by getting your cat used to sitting before feeding. This is something that the rest of your family members must be aware of.

Another serious mistake you need to avoid is to give your cat too many treats. While treats are an effective way of rewarding your cat whenever it does something positive such as following instructions, giving too many treats negates the value of training. You need to use treats sparingly. Restrict dispensing of treats to those occasions when your cat does something extra.

One of the costly mistakes that new cat owners make is neglecting to socialize with their pets as much as possible. Like with dogs, failure to socialize with your cat makes it fearful and it will easily develop aggressive behaviours. It is therefore appropriate to introduce your cat not only to family members but to your visitors as well.

Ocicats are both indoor and outdoor pets. Apart from venturing outdoors for play, they also spend some time outdoors for adventure. One of the mistakes you need avoid is to restrict your cat indoors. It is always good to take your cat out for walks, giving it an opportunity to climb trees, which is in its nature. Doing so allows your cat to release pent-up energy that it would otherwise channel into undesirable behaviour.

A common mistake that most cat owners commit that you also need to avoid is failure to keep their cats mentally active. Many cat owners limit themselves to socializing with their cats, forgetting that keeping their cats mentally active is also beneficial. Like with other pets, cats kept without mental activity become easily bored. Engage in play activities using cat toys. Hide such toys and let your cat find them out.

Ocicats are very adorable, which makes many Ocicat owners commit one serious mistake; failure to punish their cats when they engage in untoward behavior. Because physical punishment is likely to instill fear in your cat, consider using a harsh tone when communicating and expressing your disapproval for a behavior that does not impress you. These are just a few of the mistakes you need to avoid if you want to have a well behaved and obedient Ocicat as a pet. Failure on your part will simply mean having a pet that you cannot control, which will be a recipe for serious problems at home.

Chapter 7 – Care For Your Ocicat

Basic Care

Like with all cats, your Ocicat depends on you for everything, including basic care. Although your cat is independent to some extent, you are still obligated to provide it with suitable and healthy food, shelter, veterinary care, training and love. It is only with appropriate basic care that you will be able to develop a strong and rewarding relationship with your cat.

Apart from necessities such as food and shelter, proper hygiene is mandatory as part of basic care. Your cat needs to be in a clean environment at all times. Do ensure that all equipment including litter box, food/water dishes, playing toys and the room remains clean all the time. Cats are generally clean pets so do not be surprised if your cat avoids the litter box, feeding and its room if you fail to maintain good hygiene.

Basic care also involves your cat's safety. Being an indoor and outdoor cat, you need to know where your cat is at all times. This is when cat collars and ID tags become useful just in case your cat wonders off and gets lost.

Just in the same way that you and your family members visit your physician for regular check-ups, your cat also needs to visit a vet for regular check-ups. You do not need to wait for your cat to show signs of illness to take it to a vet. It is during such check-ups that minor signs of illnesses can be diagnosed and proper treatment administered. This is one of the most important basic care routines that you cannot ignore when you want to have a healthy Ocicat as a pet.

Closely related to regular check-ups is feeding. Failure to feed your cat on nutritious food can easily lead to cat medical problems. You need to avoid the practice by some cat owners who feed their cats on dog food. Cat nutritional requirements differ in a big way from dog nutritionl needs and feeding your cat on dog food simply denies your cat vital nutritional supplies.

Grooming is a very important part of your cat's basic care. You still need to groom your Ocicat even though it has characteristic short hair. Doing so is very effective in reducing the development of hairballs and matting. In addition to grooming, you also need to clip your cat's claws.

Training your cat is a very important part of basic care. By their nature, cats generally know how to do their own thing, which, regrettably, may not be proper. Training your cat from the earliest opportunity goes a long way in preventing habits such as jumping on the kitchen counter, scratching the couch and eating plants. Note that it is through training that your cat comes to learn about applicable house rules.

Although cats generally know how to entertain themselves, Ocicats in particular can be very playful. It is therefore very important that you regularly engage your Ocicat in play activities by using cat toys and other suitable items. Engaging your cat in play activities provides valuable benefits including strengthening your relationship. Furthermore, playing with your cat on a regular basis provides it with both the physical strength and mental stimulation it needs.

Giving your cat basic care can indeed be beneficial to you since you will prevent common cat diseases that can otherwise be costly when you have to take your cat to a vet for treatment. It is also by giving your cat proper basic care that you get to have a well behaved cat at home as a pet.

Living Quarters

Your cat's living quarters is its most important location. Although your Ocicat obviously ventures into other rooms and in particular the living room, there are times when it will naturally retreat back to its living quarters. This is usually the time when it needs to catch a nap or simply relax. This makes it very important to know how to treat its living quarters.

Whether you have enough room at home and have designated a room for your Ocicat or just created a special place in one of the rooms as your cat's living quarters, the room or space needs to be as clean as possible. You need to maintain cleanliness in the room or space as much as possible to make your cat feel comfortable. That cleanliness extends to ensuring that the litter box(s) and everything else in the room or space remain clean.
Just in the same way that you arrange your rooms in the best way possible, you need to ensure that your cat's living quarters is properly arranged. Do ensure that the litter box is far away from feeding/water dishes. The scratching post should also be strategically located for your cat to find it easily to perform its scratching ritual.

Grooming

"The only self-cleaning thing in this house is the cat". This is a very common phrase used on many refrigerator magnets and for good reason. By their nature, cats are the epitome of cleanliness and will go to great lengths to ensure that they remain clean at all times. This is why you observe your Ocicat "licking" its paws and other parts of the body.

The licking is not actual licking. It is actually a means by which your cat cleans itself, using the tongue as a washcloth. Cats have a unique tongue; it is barbed, making it useful for a number of purposes. It uses its tongue as a grooming tool, using it to remove loose fur, in stripping away the scent of food, in getting rid of parasites, for increasing blood circulation and for controlling its body temperature. Your cat naturally applies saliva on its forepaw before embarking on the grooming routine.

The onset of self-grooming starts right when a cat is born. The mother naturally "licks" its kitten to not only keep them clean but to also arouse them to suckle, to stimulate them to remove body waste (feces and urine) and to provide them with comfort, especially when it is hot. For the kittens, self-grooming starts when they are about four weeks old.

It is very important to know how your cat grooms itself to enable you to know how you will groom it. When self-grooming, your cat applies saliva to the inside part of one paw before cleaning itself in an upward circular pattern. It naturally starts by cleaning its nose before proceeding to the eyes, backside of the ears and eventually the forehead. Your cat does the same with the right paw. It is only after this that your cat embarks on grooming other parts of the body, such as its front legs, shoulders, flanks, genital area, hind legs and the tail. This can be a time-consuming exercise that can last for up to an hour.

The importance that cats attach to self-grooming makes it very necessary that you too come in to groom your cat. The Ocicat, just like other cat breeds, enjoys grooming. Grooming your cat does not only make it clean; doing so also goes a long way in developing a strong bond between you and your cat in addition to allowing you to screen for any visible skin problems.

There are several ways to groom your cat and one of these is brushing. Although Ocicats do not have long fur, you need to frequently brush your cat to prevent the development of hairballs, which in extreme cases require surgery to remove. Brushing your Ocicat once every week should be enough. You need to invest in a quality de-shedding tool whose use requires gentle strokes so as to prevent pain. You also need to have a soft grooming brush to use alongside a de-shedding tool.
Removing mats from your cat's body is a very important part of grooming. Although Ocicats are generally not prone to mats due to their short fur, it is good to keep your cat on the safe side by removing mats in case you notice any. Mats can be extremely painful to a point where your cat will not be able to move. Although frequent brushing reduces the risk of mats, you need to invest in quality clippers just in case.

Ensuring that your cat's ears and eyes are clean through grooming is very important. You need to examine your cat's eyes and ears for any signs of debris that you need to clean out to prevent build up. The ears are particularly prone to the build up of wax, so you need to remove it frequently. Cotton balls that are effective in cleaning both the eyes and ears. You do however need to be careful when cleaning your cat's ears. Restrict yourself to cleaning visible areas only.

Although your cat naturally indulges in its natural habit of scratching at the scratching post, you still need to examine its nails to ensure that they remain as short as possible. Make it a habit to trim your cat's nails only once a month using a quality clipper.

One area you need to avoid reaching when clipping is the triangular area of the paw that is usually pink in colour. Referred to as the quick, cutting into this area leads to bleeding, which can make it very difficult to clip your cat's nails next time since it will naturally develop fear.

It is important to note that you only need to clip the front paws. The hind paws rarely grow long.
Unlike dogs, cats rarely need bathing. It is however important that you bathe your Ocicat at least once a week. It is also during

bathing that you can effectively use your cat brush to smoothen and straighten its fur. You need to invest in quality medicated soap, shampoo and conditioner for bathing.

Grooming Products
There are a good number of cat grooming tools on the market that you need to invest in to make your cat clean, healthy and comfortable. These include brushes, flea/tick combs, sprays, shampoos, conditioners, clippers, scissors and lint removal tools. Some of the notable brands include Andis, Bio-Groom, Evercare and Oyster among other brands.

Although ignored by some cat owners, taking time to groom your Ocicat is very important. You need to set apart at least an hour once a week to groom your cat. This is so because Ocicats have short fur and therefore enjoy grooming.

Transportation
Cats and Ocicats in particular make valuable pets. Not only are they adorable and make good companions; they cheer you up when you are down in addition to making you remain active as you engage them in play. Unlike other cat breeds that are not fond of travelling, Ocicats are very outgoing and love new environments. You need to note that travelling with your Ocicat in a car can make it very uncomfortable and most likely to vomit, pee and possibly get dehydrated, which can make your journey a very disappointing one.

You need to invest in a good cat carrier in order to transport your cat without any problems. A carrier you buy should be spacious enough to allow your cat to stand, turn around and stretch. It should also be very comfortable. The best way to transport your cat using a carrier is to have your cat get used to it several days before you travel.

As part of transport preparation, it is recommended that you consult with your vet for appropriate transport advice especially when you plan to travel with your cat over a long distance. Your vet will be able to prescribe medications and sprays that will calm your cat during the journey, in effect eliminating stress, which affects cats when being transported.

Food usually plays a major role in the comfort of a cat when travelling in a car. Your cat is most likely to vomit if you feed it just minutes before you embark on a journey. It is recommended that you feed your cat at least two hours before you set off to prevent vomiting. One serious mistake you need to avoid when travelling with your cat in a car is to let it out when you stop along the way. Your cat will become confused and possibly run away. Only let it out if you have a leash.

Exercises

Ocicats are very good indoor and outdoor cats. Even so, you still need to subject your cat to different exercises. Depending on the type of food, how frequently you feed your Ocicat and the kind of treats you give it, your cat can easily gain excess body weight, which is a foundation for serious health conditions.

The only effective way to help your cat in maintaining a healthy body weight is through exercise. Exercising your cat is also beneficial even if it does not gain excess body weight. Exercising your cat goes a long way in ensuring that it remains physically fit.

By their nature, Ocicats are very flexible animals and can perform different types of exercises. One of the simple exercises you may consider subjecting your cat to is by use of laser pointer. Moving the laser around at different heights gives your cat a good opportunity to stretch as it moves to paw the light on a wall.

You definitely cannot ignore the importance of a cat tree when it comes to exercising your cat. Having a cat tree gives your cat a good opportunity to exercise as it climbs it. The other benefit of having a cat tree lies in the fact that you do not need to be around for your cat to exercise; it can do so even in your absence. In the absence of a cat tree, you need to ensure that there are no obstructions to windows to allow your cat jump on the windows as it pleases.

Having plenty of cat toys is beneficial to your cat in terms of exercise. Because of their playful nature, you need to have different types of cat toys that allow for different types of exercises. You may alternatively use readily available items at home instead of buying.

Many cat owners have of late found their treadmill valuable in exercising their cats and you too may consider the same if you happen to have one at home. Although your cat will learn quickly on how to walk and run on the mill, you will need to supervise it very closely.

One form of exercise you cannot ignore is taking your cat out for walks occasionally. A simple walk along the road or in a park exposes your cat to a new environment, which in itself provides for additional psychological benefits.

Cat Toys

Ensuring that your Ocicat exercises on a regular basis is very important and there is no better way to do so than with cat toys. Cat toys provide the opportunity for your cat to exercise both body and mind. Not only does your cat's body remain physically fit; its mental health is also enhanced, in the process relieving stress in addition to improving blood circulation within the body. Cat toys are also very effective in training a cat to abandon retrogressive behavior while at the same time acquiring progressive behaviors.

There are basically four types of cat toys that you need to invest in:

Wand Toys

A wand toy does not need to be a special item. You can make use of a stick or a piece of cloth. Twitching (stick) or waving (cloth) in circles has the positive effect of enticing your cat. This is because such an item's movement becomes similar to potential prey. You can add other enticing items on the wand to make it not only attractive but encouraging for your cat to keep on playing. Other items you can add on the wand include coloured feathers.

It is very important that you keep the wand away from the cat once play session is over. Your cat should not get used to the wand because that may negate its usefulness during play. It will be similar to a cat getting used to a prey to a point that it does noting when the prey passes by. There are different wand brands on the market if you choose to buy.

Ball Toys

Balls are very effective as cat toys. Unlike ordinary balls however, cat ball toys are small. To your cat, the movement of these balls on the floor resembles the scampering of potential prey, which entices your cat to a point that it chases after the balls. Like with a wand toy, a good way to effectively make use of cat balls is to add some niceties on the balls, niceties that your cat will strive to chase and grab. You have the option of buying ping-pong balls, sponge balls or Mylar balls among other balls.

Food-Dispensing Toys

These are the best toys to have when you plan to leave your cat at home for a long time on any given day. These toys literally deliver the food to your cat whenever it engages in play with them. One great benefit of these toys is that they teach your cat to work for its food, with the work being the play activity. This engages its mind, teaching it new tricks in the process. You can indeed make use of cat treats with these toys. Like with the other toys, there are different brands of food-dispensing ball toys on the market that you can choose from.

Catnip Toys
Catnip is a stimulating herb that cats really enjoy eating. Catnip toys are designed in such a way that they allow you to stuff catnip in them. The amount of catnip you stuff in is very critical because your cat can be over-stimulated.

Regardless of which cat toys you decide to buy, the toys should be those that stimulate your cat's natural instincts. The toys should mimic prey to encourage your cat to not only engage in play more but to act on its natural instincts.

Caring for a Pregnant Ocicat

Although you have the option of buying a spayed Ocicat kitten/cat, you may also choose to buy one not subjected to the procedure, in which case it is bound to become pregnant when a partner is available or when you take it to a vet for that specific purpose. Caring for a pregnant Ocicat, just like with caring for any pregnant cat, differs greatly from caring for a non-pregnant cat in many respects.

From the onset, you need to know whether or not your cat has attained pregnancy. This should be at the earliest possible opportunity so that you adjust a number of things to suit its condition. Generally, a cat's gestation period ranges between 60 and 70 weeks and although you are not able to ascertain whether or not your cat is pregnant through urine or blood tests, there are specific signs you need to be on the lookout for.

The first sign of a cat's pregnancy is what is usually referred to as pinking up. This is the enlargement of a cat's nipples in which case the nipples not only become enlarged but become pinkish in colour as well. You are able to notice this when your cat is about three weeks pregnant.

Like in human females, pregnant cats gain weight naturally when pregnant. You will notice a gradual increase in body weight when you hold your cat and notice the pregnancy if you are keen. Increase in body weight usually occurs at the same time that pinking up occurs.

Another simple and clear sign of cat pregnancy that can help you know whether or not your cat is pregnant is morning sickness, just in the same way it happens to human females when they attain pregnancy. Clears sign of morning sickness in cats manifest in excessive sleep, especially during morning hours, and failure to eat or avoid certain food stuffs.

It is important that you take your cat to a vet for confirmation of the pregnancy. A vet will be able to professionally ascertain your cat's pregnancy through palpitation. Even so, this will only be possible when the pregnancy is around four weeks. A vet may also opt to do an ultrasound but not X-ray in ascertaining pregnancy.

With your cat's pregnancy confirmed, you need to quickly adjust several things. Your vet should indeed be in a position to inform you about which adjustments you need to carry out, one of which is nutrition. Your pregnant cat will need an increased amount of nutritious food. The amount of food should, however, not be excessive so as to prevent labour problems when the time comes for her to give birth.

This is also the time to ensure that your cat has access to safe drinking water at all times. You also need to allow your cat have as much rest as possible. She should only be engaged in play when she initiates it. Your cat requires close monitoring during the whole period of pregnancy. Your vet will most likely advise you on when to take your cat for check-ups.

Apart from nutritious food, water and visits to the vet for check-ups, you need to buy several supplies in readiness for your cat giving birth. These include a kitten box, surgical gloves, syringe/eyedropper to aspirate nose/mouth secretions, cotton thread for ties, scissors, clean towels, antiseptic for cleaning umbilical and kitten milk replacer.

The last week of your cat's pregnancy is a very critical moment. This should be when you have introduce her to the kitten box, which you need to place in a quiet, warm location away from children. Because your cat is most likely to spend much time in her new location, you need to make food and water readily available.

There are a number of things you will notice when your cat will have gone into labour. Firstly, her mammary glands will have increased tremendously in size. She will also most likely start nesting and have a general change of behaviour.

Although you have made every effort to provide your cat with a kitten box, it can occur that your cat may choose to give birth elsewhere but within the house. This is perfectly normal and should not be a cause of concern. You will only need to transfer her and the kittens to the kitten box.

It is natural that your cat will give birth without your help. You do, however, need to watch her very closely. There are several scenarios that will require you to call the vet. These include excessive high body temperature, unpleasant smell of discharge, contractions lasting more than 20 minutes without any signs of kitten and protrusion of placenta through the vulva without any sign of kitten.

Taking care of the kitten should not be a big problem since your cat will do almost everything. You will however have specific responsibilities towards your cat. In addition to ensuring that you maintain a high level of hygiene in your cat's room or space, you will need to ensure that your cat receives a nutritious diet and supplements to properly feed the kittens. The kittens will be able to start feeding on solid food when they are between four and five weeks, with the introduction of solid food being on gradual basis.

It is only after six weeks that you can start weaning the kitten in readiness to selling them off or giving them off as gifts if you so wish. Ocicats are very social animals and it is very necessary that you socialize the kittens as much as possible. The period between eight and ten weeks of their lives is particularly important. This is the time the kittens need to be socialized, which can be by exposing them to your family members and letting them explore other spaces and rooms in the house.

One of the most important things you cannot ignore once your cat gives birth is the need to have the kittens wormed and vaccinated. Your vet should be in a position to advise you on when this should be done.

It is important to point out that although your cat can take up to between eight and ten weeks to become pregnant again, the possibility that she can attain another pregnancy at two weeks after giving birth remains high. This is one of the reasons why many cat owners choose to have their female cats spayed. You will therefore need to take precautions to prevent your cat falling pregnant again soon after giving birth, unless you intend it to be so.

One serious challenge you may face once your cat gives birth is when your cat rejects her kittens. This can be very challenging since you will have the responsibility to hand raise the kittens. Generally, Ocicats give birth to few kittens, in most cases between three and four kittens. It should not surprise you to find out that your cat has given birth to up to six kittens.

Chapter 8 – Feeding

Nutrition

Your cat requires the appropriate nutrients necessary for body development, growth and the general functioning of the body. These nutrients reside in the food that you feed your cat. Failure to feed your cat nutritious food stuffs definitely leads to specific nutrient-deficiency illnesses/diseases, some that are obviously life-threatening. Just in the same way that you pay close attention to what you eat, you also need to pay close attention to what you feed your cat and in particular the nutritional value of the food.

Of all nutrients, water is probably the most important nutrient that your cat needs, although it cannot survive on water alone. The fact that a big percentage of your cat's body weight is literally made up of water makes it very necessary that you supply your cat with fresh drinking water on a daily basis. Lack of water in the body does not only interfere with smooth metabolism; it can also be a cause of serious illnesses.

Your cat also needs a sufficient amount of protein. Protein plays a very important role in the body and in particular in the formation of body cells, tissues, enzymes, organs, antibodies, enzymes and hormones. Your cat's body also requires protein to repair body tissues and for the proper maintenance of the body.

Closely related to protein are amino acids, which your cat also requires. Amino acids are literally the building blocks of proteins and while your cat's body can easily synthesize non-essential amino acids from its diet, its body cannot naturally synthesize essential amino acids such as taurine.

Your cat does not only require water and protein. It also requires fats. Fats are very important when it comes to the production of specific hormones and in cell structure. Fats are also required by the body for the proper utilization of certain vitamins. The food you feed your cat must contain essential fats such as linoleic and arachidonic acids. Lack of these fats can easily lead to your cat suffering from reduced growth and skin problems.

As has already been indicated elsewhere, Ocicats are playful and therefore require a lot of energy to remain active. This is why you need to feed your Ocicat on carbohydrates. Carbohydrates do not only provide your cat's body with the energy it requires, carbohydrates play a critical role in maintaining good health of the intestine. You need to note that cats are generally carnivorous animals and therefore need very little carbohydrates.

Vitamins are the other very important nutrients that your cat needs. Different vitamins play different roles in the body with some vitamins required for enzyme reaction. Since your cat's body cannot synthesize most vitamins, it is very necessary that the food you feed your cat contains all the required vitamins. Like with the other nutrients, lack of vitamins leads to the occurrence of various vitamin-deficiency illnesses.

Lastly, your cat requires a sufficient supply of minerals for proper bone and teeth development, for metabolic processes and for maintenance of appropriate fluid balance within the body. Because your cat's body cannot synthesize minerals, you must ensure that your cat food contains these vital inorganic compounds.

Although your cat definitely needs different nutrients to grow and remain healthy, the amount of nutrients you feed your cat is very critical. This is so because cats require different amounts of nutrients depending on their age.

Kitten Nutrition Needs

You definitely have no role to play when it comes to providing the kittens with nutrients. Kittens obtain all the nutrients they need for their first few weeks from their mother's milk, which contains all the necessary nutrients. There are instances where the mother may not be around because of death, illness or when the mother rejects her kittens upon giving birth. In such instances, formulated commercial milk is always the best option.

Kittens generally grow very fast during the first few weeks of being born. The commercial milk you buy must therefore contain adequate amounts of all the nutrients in balanced quantities. It is important to point out that kittens do require energy three times that of adult cats and proteins two times that of adults.

Adult Cat Nutrition Needs

Meeting the nutrition needs of an adult cat can be a serious challenge. Not only should an adult cat have enough to eat but also consume a diet rich in all the necessary nutrients. An adult Ocicat is not only active and therefore requires an increased amount of energy; it also requires an increased amount of protein for repair of the body's tissues and other bodily functions. It also requires an increased amount of essential fats particularly during cold weather. Although it is very necessary that you feed your cat on these, you need to be careful so as not to make your cat obese.

It is very important to note that although your adult cat will need the same amount of nutrients during adulthood, there are exceptions. Periods when your cat is sick or pregnant will definitely raise the need to buy food containing the amount of nutrients necessary, taking into account your cat's condition.

Old Cat Nutrition Needs

Just in the same way that feeding kittens and adult cats differs, feeding an old cat also differs. You are most likely to start noticing your Ocicat's aging signs when it is about fifteen years old. Because of the body composition, metabolic and immunologic changes it is bound to go through, the occurrence of age-related diseases/health conditions such as loss of muscle mass, arthritis, obesity and dental problems among others become common.

Taking into account the changes in an old cat's body and the likelihood of development of the indicated diseases/health conditions, a diet for an old cat should be one that promotes good health and appropriate body weight. Such a diet should ideally be low on carbohydrates but high on proteins, vitamins, essential fatty acids and minerals.

The Right Food

You have two options when it comes to the right food for your cat; canned and dry food, which at times is referred to as dry kibble. Compared with canned food, dry food stuffs have low water content, high carbohydrates and are high in plant protein. Considering that cats are carnivorous animals, dry kibble is not the right food for your cat.

Although your cat needs food rich in protein, it is better off with animal-based protein. Feeding your cat plant-based protein derived from vegetables simply has no value to your cat in terms of nutrition. Unlike plant-based protein, animal-based protein contains amino acids, the essential fats that are beneficial to your cat. Canned food contains animal-based protein, making canned food the right food for your cat.

Although canned food cannot be said to be that fresh, dry kibble goes through a lot of processing in addition to being cooked at high temperatures for long times. This does not only lower thr quality of the protein within but also damages other nutrients.

The benefit of canned cat food over dry kibble is also in the amount of water contained. Cats generally do not drink water since their prey in the wild supplies them with enough water. Having a cat at home therefore requires that you feed it on a diet rich in water, which makes canned food the right food for your cat.

You have two options when it comes to cat food. The first option is to prepare cat food on your own at home or buy commercial canned foods. It is important to look at these two options to enable you to make the right decision when it comes to food for your cat.

Unknown to some cat owners, cats are carnivorous animals and therefore rely on eating raw meat. Whether it is fresh or raw meat does not matter since wild cats kill their prey and may not consume the whole prey in one instance. Cat owners who have a negative view on feeding their cats on raw meat therefore deny their cats what they are actually supposed to eat. A common belief by such cat owners usually has to do with the element of food poisoning.

Unlike us humans who are highly susceptible to food poisoning, cats are not. This is because while the food we eat resides in our intestines for anything between 35 and 55 hours, the food that a cat eats only resides in its intestine for between 12 and 16 hours. This simply means that any harmful bacteria remain within a cat's intestine for a short period of time, unlike in humans. The short period of time therefore lowers the risk of food poisoning.

It is therefore perfectly in order to buy raw meat to feed your cat on. Even as you do so, you need to remember that not all raw meat sources are the same in quality. You need to consider buying whole cuts of meat that you can thoroughly clean before feeding your cat instead of buying pre-ground meats available in supermarkets.

It can be very fulfilling if you opt to prepare cat's food at home. Even if you do so, it is very important that you do not subject your cat to the same meat source. You seriously need to consider changing meat sources. You have the option of feeding your cat on beef, rabbit meat or chicken among others. You also need to consider adding in some water and recommended supplements.

The second option is to go for commercial cat food and in this case canned cat foods. There is however a serious challenge you are likely to face when shopping for canned cat food; marketing gimmicks or food labels. Some of the food labels you are most likely to come across on canned cat foods include "For Indoor-Only Cat", "Natural", "Premium", "Breed Specific", Veterinarian Recommended" and "Therapeutic Diet" among other labels.

Although they seem very promising, some of the food labels can be very misleading. The reality is that most canned foods with these labels contain wheat, corn, soy and by-products. While wheat, corn and soy definitely have high levels of carbohydrates that your cat does not really need, the by-products happen to be the only source of protein for your cat, which is not appropriate.

The only effective way to overcome the challenge presented by promising yet false food labels is to look at both the composition and ingredients used in making canned cat food when shopping. While the composition part of it refers to the percentage of fat, protein and carbohydrates, ingredients refer to the specific nutrients in the food. You need to pay attention to three important things when it comes to choosing the right canned cat food; it should be food that is high in water content, low in carbohydrates and contains animal-based protein instead of plant-based protein.

It is worth pointing out that mainstream canned cat foods can at times be very expensive, depending on your location. This is because they do contain muscle meat of chicken and turkey among others, which is normally listed as the first ingredient. Depending on your financial position, you may consider buying canned cat foods that contain by-products. These are normally labeled as "chicken by-products" or "turkey by-products" among others. The fact that they are affordable does not mean that they are of no nutritional value.

Like with all canned foods, canned cat foods do feature preservatives and ascertaining the kind of preservative used in cat food is very important. There are canned cat foods that contain such preservatives as ethoxyguin, BHA and BHT. These are chemicals that have been proved to be unsafe when used as preservatives. Although most cat food manufacturers have abandoned the use of such preservatives, you need to check to ensure that the canned cat food you are about to buy does not contain them.

Feeding Program
There is really no uniform cat feeding program. This is the frequency at which you need to feed your cat. How frequently

you feed your Ocicat kitten, adult cat or old cat definitely differs. This is because they need to be fed at different intervals and in different amounts at every stage of their life. Your home environment and type of food you feed your cat on also informs feeding frequency.

Just like with human babies, kittens need to be fed small amounts of food at regular intervals. This is because their tummies are not yet capable of handling large amounts of food yet this is the time that they need a sufficient amount of various nutrients necessary for growth and development. Kittens generally need to be fed at least four meals spread out in any given day.

Unlike kittens that need to eat nutritious food for growth and development, your adult Ocicat needs to eat maintenance food. This is food that does not only aid in further development of the body but in maintaining strong healthy bones and in enhancing the body's immune system. Because it can be difficult to ascertain the amount of food that your adult cat needs, it is better to let it eat until it is satisfied. Two meals in any given day should be enough.

Just in the same way that feeding kittens differs from feeding adult cats, feeding an old Ocicat also differs. Old cats are generally susceptible to various diseases and health conditions that make it necessary to tailor your adult cat's feeding frequency, taking into account any health problems it may have. The same goes for sick kittens and adult cats.

It is important to look at the feeding program for adult cats because this is the cat you are most likely to have. You have two options when it comes to designing a feeding program for your cat. Your first option is to let your cat get used to a free feeding program where you fill its feeding dish with a large amount of food that it can eat when it wishes. Although this program best suits a cat that is often left alone at home for a considerable amount of time, it has its disadvantages. Firstly, you are obligated to buy kibble cat food because fresh food may not last long in the open. Secondly, there is the risk of your cat over-eating and therefore developing obesity.

Your other option is to design a scheduled feeding program where your cat gets used to a specific time when it is served food. This program can be very beneficial considering the fact that you are literally in a position to control how much food your cat consumes at any given time.

The fact that you have designed a feeding program for your cat should not mean that such a program is permanent. There is always room to alter a program depending on different situations such as when travelling, when your cat is sick, when your cat is pregnant (if a female and not spayed) and when adverse weather changes occur.

Food Allergies
Just like it is with humans, cats too develop different allergies including inhalant, flea bite and food allergies. In the case of food, cats generally develop a food allergy when subjected to specific food stuff on a regular basis. Ocicats do develop allergies when they are between two and six years old, although a few have been noted to develop food allergies as early as when they are five months old and when they are as old as twelve years old.

Contrary to a popular belief, a food allergy does not necessarily mean food intolerance. Unlike food intolerance that manifests itself in the form of diarrhoea and/or vomiting, a food allergy exhibits real symptoms that may include itchy skin, hair loss and excessive scratching among other symptoms.

Causes of food allergies in cats are usually specific ingredients found in cat foods and in particular in cat food stuffs such as corn, soy, dairy products, wheat and seafood. It is worth noting that these are the same food stuffs found in dry or kibble cat foods.

Determining whether or not your cat suffers from a food allergy can be a very big challenge. This is because food allergy symptoms are in most cases similar to those presented by cat diseases/health conditions like flea bite allergy and intestinal parasite hypersensitivity. There are however several ways through which you can determine whether or not your cat suffers from a food allergy or other disease, although determination can take some time.

The most effective way through which you can determine whether or not your cat suffers from food allergy is to undertake food trial. This means subjecting your cat to a specific type of food for several days while looking out for any allergy symptoms. It is important to note that blood tests are only effective in diagnosing other types of allergies but not food allergy.

There are instances where your cat's food allergy and associated symptoms become serious. This is usually the time to take your cat to a vet for examination and treatment. Your vet will most likely feed your cat fatty acids, steroids and prescribe antihistamines as the first line of treatment. The only effective way of treating food allergy in cats is the avoidance of causative food.

What Not to Feed Your Ocicat

Food that is edible for you and/or your dog may not be edible for your cat. Feeding your cat on certain food stuffs can not only cause allergies and intoxication, but consumption of certain food stuffs can easily lead to your cat going into a coma with increased risk of instant death.

It is perfectly normal to have alcoholic beverages at home so long as you keep them safe and away from your cat. Your cat will definitely be intoxicated when it consumes any food containing alcohol and can easily go into a coma with high chances of dying.

Spices make food very tasty but only for humans. Feeding your cat spices can cause a serious allergic reaction and toxicity, which can lead to death.

Cats are carnivorous animals and therefore do well with meat but not bones. Whether from fish, beef, lamb or poultry, bones are simply dangerous to your cat. Not only can they cause obstruction; bones can also lacerate your cat's digestive system and cause serious problems.

You should not feed or let your cat feed on food such as tea, chocolate, coffee and caffeine. These contain caffeine, theophylline and theobromine. These are ingredients that cause vomiting and other health problems in cats.

While human vitamin and mineral supplements can indeed be healthy, they can be very dangerous when you feed your cat them. You need to keep all your food supplements far from the reach of your cat.

These are just a few of food stuffs that you should not feed your cat. Although your cat will naturally avoid some of these food stuffs, you need to safely keep away those that it can accidentally consume.

Cat Treats

Giving your cat treats occasionally is highly recommended. Contrary to common belief by some cat owners, cat treats are not entirely valueless. Modern cat treats are formulated to encourage good dental, digestive, general and skin health, depending on the type of treat you buy. Note that there are crunchy, dental, soft, catnip/grass and jerky cat treats. You also have the option of buying grain-free, natural or organic cat treats. To enhance their appeal and taste, cat treats are in most cases flavoured. You may choose to buy beef, chicken, vegetarian, turkey, tuna or fish flavoured treats.

Your cat definitely needs the intake of calories that cat treats provide. However, it is very important that you measure the amount of treats you feed your cat. Because cat treats largely contain calories, they should not make up more than 10% of your cat's calorie intake. Your cat should obtain the remaining 90% from good quality nutritious foods.

Like with shopping for canned cat food, it is important that you choose cat treats with utmost care. This is because some information contained on cat treat labels may not be correct. You seriously need to look out for the amount of calories a cat treat food contains before you buy.

When to feed your cat treats is very important. This is because there is increased risk of your cat developing addiction or a taste for treats instead of its regular foods. Because of this, you need to feed your cat treats at special occasions only. This can be when it does something positive like mastering a rule and excelling in an exercise or training.

Because cat treats contain a lot of calories, they are not recommended for overweight cats. Feeding your overweight cat treats will simply worsen its condition and increase the risk of serious health conditions. For an overweight cat, go for Catnip/grass treats. Both are cereal grasses and therefore low in calories.

You should be able to find different types of cat treats on the market. There are those that are soft and moist and those that are hard, just similar to dry cat food. Your cat will most likely hate dry treats in favour of soft treats. It is always a good idea to balance between the two for your cat to receive all the nutrients it needs for good health.
There are a number of cat treat brands on the market and just like with choosing canned food carefully, you need to choose cat treats carefully. The most important things to look into are the ingredients a treat is composed of. This is very necessary because some cat treats may contain ingredients that may cause allergies.

How you store the cat treats you buy is of great importance. The Ocicat is a very clever cat and will notice when you feed it on treats. It will therefore look for them where you store the canned food. It may develop the habit of stealing treats if you fail to store them in a secure place. The best way to go about storing cat treats is to store the same in a different location from where you store its regular food.

Chapter 9 – Training

Cat Training

Cat training refers to the practice of instilling certain values in your cat. It is a wide area that also involves changing some of your cat's natural but unpleasant behaviour. Cat training provides several benefits not only to you but to your cat as well. A well trained cat usually has its body and mind well stimulated, which goes a long way in enhancing its overall health. Well trained cats also exhibit good behaviour, especially in the presence of visitors. It is also through training that you build a close relationship with your cat. Failure to give your cat the necessary training can easily turn your cat into a pest instead of a pet.

Cat training requires that you first understand your cat in different respects. Luckily, Ocicats are not only highly intelligent but also very easy to train. You can easily train your Ocicat to stop doing something or to behave in a certain manner at certain times. Like other animals, cats do learn through experience. Your Ocicat will stop doing something from which it has had a bad experience.

You have two options when it comes to training your cat. You have the option of taking your cat to a dedicated cat or pet training centre/invite a cat or pet trainer to your home or undertake the training on your own. Because taking your cat somewhere else or engaging the service of a trainer involves expenses, you may consider undertaking the training on your own. Training your cat personally can be very fulfilling, especially when you see your cat positively responding to your instructions.

One thing you must avoid at all costs when training your cat is punishment. Unlike dogs, cats respond negatively to reprimands and punishments. Punishing or reprimanding your cat for failing to follow given instructions instills fear in your cat, which makes training very difficult. Furthermore, a fearful cat will always try

78

to run away. The secret to training your cat effectively lies in using treats. Rewarding your cat with treats whenever it does something positive or when it responds positively and follows given instructions is the only sure way to give your cat proper training. There are three basic areas your cat needs to be trained in; house training, behavioural training and trick training.

House Training

You will share almost every room in your home with your Ocicat. Although it tends to spend most of its time in its room/space or outdoors, it will on a regular basis venture into the other rooms for companionship or to simply explore the other rooms. This makes it necessary to train it properly in different areas.

Litter training is the most important house training that you must give your cat. You must however ensure that the litter box is not only clean at all times but placed in the most appropriate location within the cat's room or space. One reason why cats avoid their litter box and instead choose to urinate in other places in the house is usually due to dirty litter. Note that what may seem clean to you may not necessarily be clean to a cat. You need to get accustomed to changing the litter on a daily basis before you can embark on litter training.

You need to start introducing your cat to its litter box immediately after you bring it home. Although filling the litter box with dry and clean soil will naturally attract the cat when it needs to go, you still need to introduce your cat to it. It is highly recommended that you place the litter box away from the cat's sleeping quarters and feeding/water dishes. Apart from litter box training, you need to train your cat on where to sit or lie when in the living room.

Behavioural Training

Behavioural training is probably the most extensive and difficult part of cat training. This is because of the many behavioural changes you need to train your cat to adopt or discard.

Your cat has natural hunting instincts and will naturally bite or claw your hands when you engage in play activities. Although this is normal cat behaviour, you need to train your Ocicat to abandon this behaviour. The best way to offer the training is during play sessions where you stop play immediately when it bites or claws. This is also the best time to use treats, denying your cat them when it engages in biting and clawing.

Your action of stopping playing and denying it treats sends a strong message to the cat that it is because of its behaviour that play has not only stopped but it has been denied treats as well. You are most likely to notice change in this behaviour during play sessions that follow when your cat resorts to using its paws instead of teeth and nails during play. This is also the time to effectively make use of treats, rewarding it for not biting and clawing.

Cats do communicate by meowing. Your cat will naturally meow when hungry, when in danger, when in need of a mate (in the case of a non-spayed female cat), to attract your attention or when requesting something. Although perfectly normal, excessive meowing can be a serious problem in the house. Your first reaction to your cat's excessive meowing should be to consult your vet with the aim of ascertaining whether or not your cat suffers from illness or disease.

It is also important to note that changes in the house such as re-arranging the house can make a cat meow a lot. It is equally important to note that you may be the cause of excessive meowing if you have made your cat develop the habit of meowing by giving it something whenever it meows. The most effective way to train your cat to stop excessive meows is to give something like a treat when it is quiet and denying it a treat when it meows.

While having a playful Ocicat as a pet is perfectly in order, in can be a big challenge when you have a hyperactive and playful Ocicat. Your hyperactive cat will indulge in activities like too much play, hiding things in the house, chasing unseen mice, jumping on and off furniture and in extreme cases stealing.

Cats that do exhibit these behaviours are in most cases hyperactive cats not engaged in play activities and often left alone. The most effective way to get your cat to abandon such behaviours is to provide means such as play activities through which your cat can expend the excess energy. In the case of an un-spayed or un-neutered cat, this may also be the right time to have it neutered/spayed.

One of the most misunderstood cat behaviours by many cat owners is a cat's territorial behaviour. Like other wild cats such as Leopards, your Ocicat will naturally mark its territory within the house, which can be every room and items in the house including furniture. Note that cats have a high sense of smell and will detect any foreign smell, however light the smell may be.

Your cat has scent glands located along its tail, on its front paws, on either side of its forehead, on its chin and on its lips. Its behaviour of rubbing its tail or head on you or anything else in the house is therefore not a way of grooming itself but is a way of marking its territory by picking up smell and leaving its smell on it.

Although it's naturally normal for your cat to mark its territory, this cannot be extreme. Note that cats engage in this behaviour as one way of guarding themselves from possible threats. The scent they leave behind when marking their territory is meant to serve as a warning to other cats that the area is already occupied. The only effective way to train your cat to abandon this behaviour that at times can be irritating is to socialize with your cat as much as possible. Your cat should never feel threatened in any way.

Having an untrained cat at home as a pet can be very dangerous where you also have a bird or birds as pets. By their nature, cats have hunting and chasing instincts. Although your cat may not chase after prey, which in such a case is the bird to kill for food, it will chase out of instinct with the aim of tossing the bird around, which can result in serious injuries to the bird. This is predatory behaviour that is very common with both indoor and outdoor cats including Ocicats.

Persistent predatory behaviour stems from the fact that your cat does not have the opportunity to vent out its natural instinct and therefore directs it to the potential in-house pet. The only effective way to offer predatory training is to have your cat socialize with a potential prey under close watch. Such socialization makes the cat realize that the potential prey is indeed part of the family.

Nocturnal Training

Your Ocicat is naturally a nocturnal animal. It will spend a lot of time sleeping during the day and become active during the night when you are asleep. Its night activities can be very disturbing if you do not offer appropriate training. Your cat will naturally become active from late in the evening to the early morning.

Letting your cat get used to this schedule will deny you quality sleep. The most appropriate training you offer should aim at changing its schedule of activities, which you can do by engaging it in play activities during the day instead of letting it sleep. Because changing its schedule can be challenging, you need to go about doing so gradually until it gets used to the new schedule.

Even so, you will still not stop your cat from engaging in night activities albeit to a smaller degree. You therefore still need to make available suitable cat toys to allow your cat to engage in some activities during the night. You do, however, need to set up the toys away from your bedroom to avoid sleep disruption.

Trick Training

One reason why Ocicats make good companions is the fact that they are receptive to trick training. You can train your Ocicat to do a number of things in the house including ringing the door bell or playing dead.

Dominance Training

Although your cat is naturally independent and can easily defend itself against attacks by other cats, there are times when dominance training becomes necessary. It is through dominance training that your cat gains the confidence it needs when in the presence of other cats. This training is particularly useful in case you live in an area with many other cats in the neighbourhood and your cat ventures out a lot.

Command Training

This is one of the most important trainings you have to subject your cat to. Your cat should be able to positively respond to commands such as come, roll, go and sit. This training requires a lot of time and patience on your part because your cat will obviously not master all the commands you give in one training session.

Leash Training

Walking on a leash is the other important training you must offer your cat. This is because you will occasionally take your cat out for walks. Because cats are generally not receptive to leashes, you need to expose it to the leash long before you embark on leash training. It is highly recommended that you place the leash near its food dish or other favourite location where it sees it often and gets used to it. It pays to only buy a harness specially designed for cats.

Training Rules

- Regardless of the type of training, be patient but committed to your cat's training schedule.
- Never resort to punishing your cat in case it fails to perform as expected. Punishing it will make it develop fear and therefore fail to master any training that you offer.
- It pays to embark on training at a slow pace, train slowly to do one thing until it has mastered it, then move on to the next.

- Always reward your cat whenever it performs better for encouragement.
- Set a specific training time every day. This will get your cat accustomed to the training routine.

Chapter 10 – Health

Ocicat Health

The Ocicat breed is not only people-oriented, it is also one of a few cat breeds not susceptible to many health challenges, something the breed borrows from the Abyssinian breed. It is partly because of Ocicat's good health that most live beyond their general life expectancy of 15 years. This is as long as proper care, recommended feeding and necessary vaccinations are given. Even so, there are several diseases and health conditions that the Ocicat is susceptible to. Most of the diseases and health conditions are not hereditary but acquired.

Common Illnesses/Diseases

Gingivitis - Gingivitis is a periodontal disease. It causes inflammation of the gums that turn reddish. Plaque formation also occurs. Plaque is basically a collection of debris, food, dead skin, mucous and bacteria. The gingival surface however remains very smooth. The disease can easily be reversed at the earliest stage through proper dental care.

Without proper dental care, the disease develops further with occurrence of calculus under the gums. Calculus is a mixture of organic matter, carbonate and calcium phosphate. In addition to the further development of plaque, the gum surface becomes irregular with some pain in the gums.

As the disease progresses, it forms a narrow space between the teeth and the inner wall of the gum. The bacteria present in this space mutate and release toxins that damage gingival tissue. Occurrence of gingivitis is common not only in cats but also in dogs aged three years and above.

Apart from the swelling and reddishness of the gums, other symptoms of the disease include bad breath. Gingivitis is largely caused by the accumulation of plaque. There are also other risk factors that encourage the occurrence of the disease. These include excessive soft food, old age, bad chewing habits, diabetes, breathing through the mouth, crowded teeth and autoimmune disease among other risk factors.

Because of the danger that gingivitis poses to your cat, you need to help your cat in preventing the occurrence of the disease. This you can do by ensuring that your cat's oral health remains at its optimum by brushing its teeth at least twice a week with veterinarian toothpaste or using a finger pad to clean the teeth. This simple action goes a long way in preventing the build-up of plaque.

A serious case of gingivitis requires veterinarian attention at the earliest possible time. In addition to physical examination, your vet will, as a matter of routine, try to establish possible causes of the disease, which can be the kind of food you feed your cat.

There are several ways through which your vet may choose to treat the disease, depending on his/her findings. Your vet may prescribe antibacterial solution for squirting on your cat's teeth to prevent the build-up of plaque, prescribe dietary supplements or prescribe specific foods that help in promoting good dental health.

In cases of serious gingivitis, your vet may choose to remove baby (deciduous) teeth that may cause teeth overcrowding, which is a cause of the disease, or remove particularly affected teeth. It is also possible that your vet may choose to only remove plaque and calculus before polishing the teeth's surface.

Gingivitis is a serious gum disease that you must not let your cat suffer from. It can reach a stage where your cat will not be able to chew food properly or even eat due to pain. You will certainly not rule out malnourishment and possible death of your pet.

Familial Amyloidosis - This is not a disease but rather a health condition that affects the liver. It is actually a group of disorders with similar characteristics; the abnormal deposition of amyloid (a fibrous protein) into the body's tissues. Amyloid occurs as a hard and waxy substance and develops as a result of the degeneration of tissue. The disposition interferes with the normal functioning of areas where the protein has reached. Familial Amyloidosis is a hereditary health disorder common in Abyssinian, Burmese and Siamese breeds of cats.

Although this is a hereditary disorder, it can also be caused by various factors including chronic infection, inflammation of the inner layer of the heart caused by bacterial endocarditis and tumours. The condition presents several symptoms including general body weakness, loss of appetite, excessive thirst and urination, vomiting, enlarged abdomen and swelling of the limbs accompanied by joint pain.

Familial Amyloidosis is not treatable. It is a disorder that impairs the liver, seriously affecting its function and that of other organs and most cats die from the disease. There are, however, specific measures that your vet can take to lessen the pain and help prolong your cat's life in case of infection. Your vet may take such measures as blood transfusion (blood change), fluid therapy, diet change and in some cases surgery.

Retinal Atrophy - Retinal atrophy is a non-treatable, hereditary disease common in some cat breeds including the Abyssinian and the Ocicat. The disease is also common in some dog breeds. It is the degeneration of the retina, causing gradual loss of vision, which ends in blindness. The disease presents symptoms such as decreased vision at night, dilated pupils and cataract formation among other symptoms.

Hyperthyroidism - This is an endocrine disorder whose occurrence is directly linked to over-activity of the thyroid gland, which leads to excess levels of specific hormones. These hormones play a very important role in the body; the role of controlling the metabolism. Increased levels of these hormones have the negative effect of increasing your cat's heart rate with the possibility of your cat developing a heart murmur. Without appropriate treatment, the disease easily causes heart failure, kidney damage, high blood pressure and death.

Your cat will exhibit a number of symptoms when infected. These include diarrhoea, vomiting, behavioural changes, weight loss, increased thirst and urination, body weakness, poor coat condition and rapid heartbeat among other symptoms. These symptoms may not necessarily point at hyperthyroidism because the same symptoms are presented by other cat diseases, including cat diabetes and renal failure. It is therefore very important that you take your cat to a vet once you notice any of these symptoms.

The fact that hyperthyroidism does not affect specific breeds of cats means that all cats are at risk of suffering from the disease. It mostly affects older cats and dogs. There are two main ways of treating hyperthyroidism. A treatment method a vet chooses depends on your cat's medical condition.

Your vet may choose to prescribe medications like Tapazole, whose action is not to treat but to control the disease. Your cat will however need to use prescribed medication(s) for the rest of its life. There are instances when a vet may choose to undertake surgery with the aim of removing the enlarged thyroid. The other treatment your vet may choose is to implement radioactive iodine treatment, which involves the injection of a single dose of radioactive iodine. Iodine has the positive effect of destroying the damaged part of the thyroid while leaving the normal thyroid tissues intact.

Pyruvate Kinase deficiency - Pyruvate Kinase is an enzyme whose deficiency in your cat's body leads to the impairment of red blood cells, greatly reducing the ability of red blood cells to metabolize. The inability of red blood cells to metabolize causes anemia in addition to other blood issues. Pyruvate Kinase deficiency is very common in breeds of cats like the Somali, Abyssinian and other short-haired cat breeds including the Ocicat.

Caused by defects in genes acquired at birth, Pyruvate Kinase deficiency presents symptoms such as body weakness, anemia, jaundice and increased heart rate among other symptoms. This condition is usually addressed through bone marrow transplant, which is the only treatment method available. In addition to being an expensive treatment, it is also life-threatening. Most cats that suffer from this condition die by the time they are four years old.

The indicated diseases/health conditions are just a few of the health problems that your Ocicat is susceptible to. There are however other cat diseases/health conditions that your cat may acquire depending on your environment, your cat's diet, living conditions and whether there are other cat breeds in the house/neighbourhood or not. Some of these include:

Arthritis - Arthritis refers to negative changes that occur within the joints. These changes develop when cartilage that protects different bone joints wears out, causing friction at the joints. The friction causes swelling accompanied by pain. Although the cartilage is supposed to be replaced naturally, arthritis is bound to occur when it wears out faster than it is replaced.

Just like in humans, the onset of arthritis in cats is in advanced age although middle aged cats can also suffer from the condition. The swelling and accompanying pain is usually chronic, which causes a lot of discomfort.

There is no cure for Arthritis. It can only be treated with any treatment that a vet offers, treatment that aims at lessening the pain and swelling that your cat experiences. Treatment needs to be offered at the earliest possible time so as to prevent further loss of cartilage.

Although arthritis is common in other cat breeds such as the Himalayan, Siamese and Persian cat breeds, your Ocicat can suffer from the condition due to such factors as old age, obesity, congenital defects, accidents and infection.

Arthritis has a serious effect on a cat's health. This is because it does not only make a cat uncomfortable but impairs its mobility as well. The condition presents symptoms like limited activity, stiffness in walking, limping and social withdrawal.

Although your vet will definitely prescribe medications that help in preventing swelling and managing pain, he/she is likely to recommend the most appropriate diet for your cat as the most effective treatment option. This is because food plays a very important role in your cat's overall health.

Allergic Dermatitis - Allergic dermatitis refers to conditions that affect the skin negatively. These can be caused by factors such as food allergy, parasites, hormonal imbalances and infections. One effective way to prevent allergic dermatitis in your cat is to feed it on food rich in meat-based protein, essential fatty acids and antioxidants.

There are however instances when you may need to take your cat to a vet. This is when the skin is not only rough but has wounds. Your cat's skin should be smooth and soft without any signs of flakes. Hair on the skin should also be evenly spread out.

Diabetes - Just like in humans, cats suffer from diabetes when their metabolic system cannot effectively control the amount of sugar in their blood stream. The main cause of this is usually lack of or limited production of insulin, which is produced in the pancreas. Apart from an insufficient amount of insulin, your cat is at risk of developing diabetes if it is obese, approaching old age, is a male, stressed, has a poor diet or hormonal imbalances.

Diabetes presents several symptoms including excessive thirst, rapid weight loss, loss of appetite, vomiting, increased urination and general body weakness among other symptoms.

Once diagnosed, your vet may recommend a number of ways to help your cat cope. One of the most effective ways your vet is most likely to recommend is diet. A vegetarian diet with proper nutrients is usually very effective in managing diabetes in cats.

Gastrointestinal Disorders - These disorders also include disorders of a cat's digestive system. These are disorders that hinder smooth digestion and absorption of nutrients contained in the food that your cat eats. Gastrointestinal disorders in particular interfere with both the intestine and stomach, causing pain and in some cases swelling. Some of these disorders include acute gastroenteritis, colitis, diarrhoea, constipation, irritable bowel syndrome and pancreatitis among others.

He occurrence of these disorders presents several symptoms including vomiting, flatulence, body weakness, constipation, diarrhoea and in some cases regurgitation.

Although they do not present any immediate danger, gastrointestinal and digestive disorders can become life-threatening if not addressed in good time. You need to take your cat to a vet for correct diagnosis and treatment. Treatment options available do aim at alleviating the pain and suffering that your cat experiences in addition to eliminating symptoms. One of the most effective treatment options available relates to the food that you feed your cat. Vets do recommend highly digestible foods for cats with these conditions. Other recommended food types include high soluble foods.

You will be obligated to prevent occurrence of these disorders for the benefit of your cat. This will mean ascertaining specific factors or food stuffs that may be the cause of such disorders.

Heart Disease - Your Ocicat is at risk of suffering from heart disease and like with most cat diseases, the food you feed your cat on plays a major role in preventing or encouraging the disease. There are however other factors that may cause heart disease in your cat, including old age and heartworm among other factors.

Heart disease has the negative effect of enlarging your cat's heart, making it inefficient. In effect, the heart holds more fluid than it is supposed to hold. A clever way to go about preventing excessive fluid in your cat's heart is to feed it cat food low on sodium.

Heart disease presents several symptoms, some similar to those presented by other cat diseases. These include low-pitched cough, difficulty in breathing, weight gain/loss and abdominal swelling among other symptoms.

Kidney Disease - Kidney disease is one disease that is often ignored when looking at cat diseases. All cats, regardless of breed, are susceptible to kidney disease. The kidney plays the important role of removing waste from the bloodstream in addition to regulating the amount of fluids in the body. Failure by the kidneys to play these vital roles puts a cat's life in serious danger.

Kidney disease presents different symptoms including loss of appetite, frequent vomiting, depression, poor coat appearance and frequent urination or no urination. Kidney disease can be acute or sudden and chronic or long-term. It can be caused by factors such as trauma, surgery, shock, serious blood loss, poison, drugs and infection of the kidneys.

Unlike other cat diseases that present symptoms almost immediately, symptoms associated with kidney disease only appear when a large part of the kidneys is already destroyed. It is therefore very necessary that you take your cat for regular veterinary checkups.

Urinary Tract Infections - UTIs are various infections that do affect both the bladder and urethra. Of the infections, feline idiopathic cystitis (FIC) is the most prevalent. Thought to be caused by excessive level of stress, it causes inflammation of the urinary tract in addition to forming crystals along a cat's urinary tract. Such crystals are in most cases those of calcium oxalate.

92

UTIs present different symptoms including inappropriate urination, straining during urination, loss of bladder control, coloured urine, licking of the genitals, loss of appetite and lack of interest in any activity among other symptoms.

UTIs can be caused by several factors including obesity, diet composed of foods rich in magnesium, calcium, phosphorous and protein (unbalanced), surgery and infections. Any UTI can be very problematic since the reoccurrence rate remains high after treatment. This becomes real when the causative factor is not addressed before treatment is offered. Vets emphasize the need to feed your cat the right cat food that is not only nutritious but also well balanced.

Obesity - Acquisition of food in the wild for any creature including cats is not an easy task. Cats in the wild have to hunt and chase after their prey to feed on. The physical exertion definitely takes a toll on their bodies and it is therefore not easy to find an obese cat in the wild. Things are different, however, for domesticated cats including Ocicats. Domesticated cats have it very easy when it comes to food simply because all that they eat is readily provided, which poses the risk of obesity.

From study findings of a research study conducted by the Association for Pet Obesity Prevention (APOP) in 2011, over 50% of cats in the USA were found to be either obese or overweight. It therefore simply means that your Ocicat is also at risk of becoming obese even though it is one of the most active cat breeds you can find.

Simply put, your Ocicat is most likely to become obese when its energy intake is more that the amount of energy it uses. Just like in humans, its body converts the extra energy it consumes into fat, which gets deposited in specific locations within its body. Getting rid of deposited fat can be a big challenge, even with regulation of energy intake.

Living with an obese Ocicat or any cat for that matter can be very expensive. This is so because obesity forms the foundation of a wide range of diseases and health conditions that will see you in and out of a vet's clinic on a regular basis. Just like in humans, obesity in cats causes diseases such as arthritis, heart disease, diabetes, cancer of the bladder and breathing difficulties.

The ideal weight of your Ocicat should be between 9-14 pounds (4-6 kg) and between 6-9 pounds (3-4 kg) for a male and female respectively. You need to take anything beyond these as a cause of concern. It is therefore important that you have your cat weighed whenever you call at the vet for regular checkups, which should ideally include weight measurement.

You should, however, be able to tell whether your Ocicat is becoming obese or not even without weighing it. You should be able to feel your cat's backbone and ribs whenever you place your hand on its back. Not being able to feel the bones should be a clear sign of obesity.

Obesity is a serious health condition in cats. Just like in humans, obesity in cats encourages the occurrence of serious diseases/health conditions like diabetes, heart disease and cardiovascular diseases. Ensuring that your Ocicat maintains normal body weight goes a long way in preventing regular trips to a vet's clinic, which translates into reduced health care costs.

Your Ocicat can become obese for several reasons, one of which is free feeding. Most cats left free to choose when to eat often develop obesity. This is so because a free feeding program gives a cat the opportunity to overeat, in effect consuming too much food that its body does not really need. Veterinarians recommend feeding your adult cat between two to three meals a day with the amount of each meal controlled to avoid overeating. Ideally, your cat's food should be about half of a human meal.

The other main cause of obesity in cats is the intake of too many calories. Unlike humans, your cat does not have the Amylase enzyme that digests carbohydrates contained in their food. The enzyme plays the very important role of breaking down large carbohydrate molecules into smaller, absorbable units of glucose.

Furthermore, cats are not carbohydrate consumers by nature. Because most dry cat foods contain high levels of carbohydrates, you need to shop carefully for them. Any dry cat food you buy should have minimal carbohydrates, if any. It is highly recommended that you feed your cat a diet that is similar to its natural food, which makes canned cat food stuffs better. A cat's ideal diet should be high in meat-based protein and moderate fat and water.

Apart from carbohydrates and a free feeding program, the other main cause of obesity in cats is cat treats. The availability of cat treats has made many cat owners lazy when it comes to feeding their cats. Many cat owners rely on cat treats as their cats' main food. Cat treats contain high levels of carbohydrates and feeding your cat them on a regular basis puts it at great risk of becoming obese. You should only feed your cat on treats at special occasions as a way of appreciation or reward.

Unlike in humans, obesity in cats is a non-inherited health condition. Your Ocicat will only develop obesity because of what you feed it. It is therefore very necessary that you pay attention to what your cat eats and in what amounts.

Apart from food, you seriously need to ensure that your Ocicat is physically engaged on a daily basis. Exercises are very important not only for your cat's physique but also in stimulating its mind. You need to make effective use of cat toys to help your cat burn excess fat deposits in the body.

Formulating a balanced and nutritious weight loss diet should also be effective in helping your cat cut down on excess body weight just in case it has already become obese. You need to formulate a diet that is low on carbohydrates but high on meat-based protein and other nutrients, including fresh drinking water.

Pustule - Pustule in cats is what acne is to humans. Just like in humans, who suffer from acne mostly on the facial area, your cat is also likely to suffer from acne that affects its chin, although its lower lip can also be affected. Major causes of pustule in cats happen to be poor grooming (lack of it) and excess oil on the skin surface (oil produced from within the body).

Just like acne in humans, your cat is most likely to present symptoms such as black/whiteheads, swollen chin and development of nodules that can be very painful. Your cat can end up having boils as a result of pustule.

A vet will normally try to rule out such health issues as feline leprosy, allergy and skin tumour before diagnosing pustule. Confirmation of correct diagnosis is usually through fungal culture, biopsy test and skin scrapping among other procedures.

For treatment, a vet will normally prescribe antibiotics, topical creams and shampoos. Regular occurrence of pustules should be a cause of concern regarding your cat's general health. It may be necessary for a vet to undertake your cat's full health scan to ascertain the exact cause.

Hypoadrenocorticism - This is what is commonly referred to as Addison's disease in humans. This disease is mostly caused by an imbalance in the levels of both glucocorticoid (cortisol) and mineralocorticoids (aldosterone,) hormones produced in the adrenal gland. These two hormones play the very important role of maintaining your cat's good health and excess or insufficient production of them leads to serious health complications. Excess or insufficient production of the two hormones impairs the function of the kidney, gastrointestinal system, the nervous system and the cardiovascular system.

You cat will present a number of symptoms, which may include signs of depression, vomiting, bloody faeces, unexplained weight loss, general body weakness and lack of appetite among other symptoms. Apart from excess or insufficient production of the two hormones, the disease can also be caused by metastatic tumours.

A vet will normally perform elaborate laboratory tests, blood count and urinalysis test in diagnosing if your cat suffers from Addison's disease. If so, he/she may recommend that your cat remains hospitalized for intensive therapy since Addison's disease is usually an emergency case. The first line of treatment is usually giving body fluids intravenously with the aim of balancing the two hormones. Your cat will henceforth need to receive hormonal treatment throughout its life even with recovery.

Feline Asthma/Bronchiti - This is the inflammation of a cat's bronchi and bronchioles, which leads to the narrowing of airwaves. Left untreated, asthma/bronchitis presents the risk of a cat developing excess tissue within its lungs, tissues that make it very difficult for the lungs to inflate.

In both acute and chronic asthma/bronchitis cases, a cat is most likely to present such symptoms as coughing, body weakness, general body weakness, lack of appetite, breathing difficulties and skin coloration among other symptoms.

Although the exact cause of asthma/bronchitis in cats is yet to be known, your Ocicat is most likely to suffer from it if you smoke in the house, in which case your cat inhales the resultant smoke. The disease has also been linked to parasitic lung infection and in particular infection by lungworm, use of air fresheners at home and indoor chemical sprays.

Diagnosis of asthma/bronchitis in cats is usually through blood tests that also show whether it is acute or chronic. A vet may also need your cat's faecal sample to ascertain the presence of parasites. There are instances when a vet may order for X-ray imaging with the aim of ascertaining both the nature and extent of the disease.

Asthma/bronchitis in cats is usually a serious disease and your cat will most likely be given Oxygen therapy in addition to anti-

97

inflammatory medications to reduce swelling of the airwaves. A vet may recommend that your cat remains hospitalized for further investigation and monitoring.

Tyzzer Disease - This is a disease that mostly affects both kittens and young cats. It is a serious, life-threatening disease caused by Clostridium piliformis bacterium that multiplies within the intestines before entering a cat's liver, leading to serious damage of the liver.

If infected, your Ocicat will show a number of symptoms including general body weakness, signs of depression, loss of appetite, diarrhoea, low body temperature and abdominal distension among other symptoms.

Veterinarians do diagnose Tyzzer disease through laboratory tests of blood, urinalysis and blood count among other diagnosis procedures. Diagnosis of the disease is usually revealed when there is a high level of liver enzymes. There is no treatment for Tyzzer disease and affected cats die.

Capillariasis - This is a cat disease caused by Capillaria plica and Capillaria feliscati, parasitic worms. Although the parasites mostly affect a cat's urinary bladder, it can also affect its urinary tract. Your Ocicat will most likely show signs of frequent urination that can be painful, bloody urine and straining when urinating.

Diagnosis of this disease is through urinalysis, which should reveal presence of Capillaria ova. A vet may offer injection or other form of medications for treatment. The possibility of the disease recurring usually remains high especially if your cat is fond of venturing outdoors often. This is because it is outdoors where it has access to earthworms.

Hepatic Lipidosis - This is a disease of the liver that is commonly referred to as fatty liver. It is one of the most fatal diseases that affects domestic cats across the world. The liver plays the important roles of synthesizing proteins, producing digestive enzymes and detoxifying the body.

By its nature, a cat's liver cannot convert large amounts of fat into energy the way we humans do. Failure by a cat's liver to convert large amounts of fat efficiently leads to the accumulation of fat, which impairs the liver's function. Furthermore, the liver releases the accumulated fat that by then has turned yellow in the bloodstream, leading to yellowish eyes. Left untreated, a cat develops several health complications before dying of the disease.

Fatty liver can be caused by various health conditions and diseases including cancer, diabetes, kidney disease, inflammation of the pancreas and obesity among others. If affected, your Ocicat will most likely present such symptoms as yellowish eyes, unexplained, rapid weight loss, signs of depression, jaundice, vomiting, constipation and drooling of saliva.

A vet will normally perform routine laboratory tests of blood count, urinalysis and biochemistry profile in diagnosing the disease. Other imaging tools like radiography may also be performed to examine the abdomen. Your cat will most likely be hospitalized for treatment, which includes fluid therapy and vitamin B supplementation. A vet will obviously recommend an appropriate diet for your cat so as to prevent the re-occurrence of the disease.

Sporotrichosis - This is a disease caused by Sporothrix schenckii fungus found in mould and yeast. Your Ocicat can easily contract the fungus when it rubs against a surface with mould or yeast, in which case the fungus attaches to its skin before penetrating into the body. Your cat can also contract the disease when it inhales fumes from moulds.

If infected, your cat will most likely present symptoms such as skin lesions, swollen lymph glands and wounds on the head among other symptoms. This is a zoonotic disease that can be transmitted from human to animals and vice versa. It is therefore very important that you be careful when outdoors with your cat.

In particular, your cat should not venture into areas with decaying organic matter.

In addition to physical examination, a vet will normally carry out laboratory fluid tests to diagnose the disease. Your cat will most likely be hospitalized for treatment that includes administration of anti-fungal medications.

Feline Trichobezoars - This is what is referred to as hairballs. Although it is perfectly normal for your Ocicat to occasionally vomit a hairball, persistent and frequent vomiting of hairballs is usually a sign of a serious health problem.

The only evidence that your cat vomits hairballs is when you see the hairballs. These are masses of hair that are cylindrically shaped. They can form in your cat's stomach and it only vomits them out when it regurgitates.

The cause of hairballs is directly linked to how cats groom themselves. Your cat's tongue is designed in such a way that it is barbed, which makes it possible for it to groom itself with ease. In the process of grooming itself, it swallows some of the hair it removes. It is this hair that accumulates in the stomach that it vomits or regurgitates.

Frequent vomiting or regurgitation of hairballs calls for veterinary attention, who should ideally perform tests such as blood cell count, biochemistry profile and thyroid screening among other tests to diagnose hairballs.

Hairball treatment usually involves lubricating the hairballs in the stomach to make it easy for a cat to pass them out with faeces. A vet can also recommend feeding your cat some cat food that is commercially available and that control the accumulation of hair in the stomach. The best way to prevent your cat having hairballs is to groom it regularly.

Polyphagia - Polyphagia simply refers to a cat's increased appetite for food. It is a health condition where your cat simply starts demanding more food to the extent of becoming ravenous all the time. This condition can be caused by many factors and it is only appropriate that you ascertain the exact cause. Although your cat may gain weight, weight loss will be a sign that it is not well.

In addition to increased appetite, your cat will most likely develop obesity or lose weight. Causes include the onset of the aging process, the use of certain cat medications, diabetes and poor absorption of food.

Polyphagia is normally diagnosed through blood, urine tests and radiography imaging. Treatment normally takes into account the causative factor, which in case of a disease requires that a vet advises on the best management regime while treating the initial disease (causative factor).

Panosteitis - Panosteitis refers to the inflammation of bones in cats. It is a very painful health condition that affects the long bones found in a cat's legs. If affected, your Ocicat will most likely limp before becoming lame. Although this condition mostly affects large-sized cats including Ocicats, it can also affect medium-sized cats. It is, however, a treatable health condition that a cat can recover from to lead a perfectly normal life.

In addition to limping, your cat is also most likely to show other symptoms such as signs of depression, fever, anorexia and weight loss among other symptoms. While the actual cause of this health condition remains unknown, diagnosis is through X-ray imaging and blood tests. Treatment of this health condition is usually limited to pain management, in which case a vet is bound to prescribe anti-inflammatory and steroid medications.

Inflammatory Bowel Disease (IBD) - IBD is a term used to refer to several diseases and health conditions that affect a cat's gastrointestinal tract and whose cause(s) remain largely unknown. One characteristic of all the diseases is that they cause inflammation of the intestines.

Your Ocicat will present several symptoms if affected. Some of these include diarrhoea, signs of depression, flatulence, abdominal pain, general body weakness, bloody stool and distressed hair on the coat.

Diagnosis of IBD is normally through laboratory tests including blood count, biochemistry profile and urinalysis. Although the cure for IBD is not available, a vet will normally institute control measures that include the stabilization of body weight, reduction of immune system response and administration of antibiotic medications.

Coprophagia - This is a health condition that normally worries cat owners. Your Ocicat may suddenly start eating its own faeces after defecating. Although the actual cause of this condition is unknown, it is thought to be as a result of both mineral and vitamin deficiency in a cat's diet.

Apart from eating its faeces, you may also observe your cat eating rocks, clay and soap among other non-edible items. Your cat will also have diarrhoea and vomit frequently.

Apart from mineral and vitamin deficiency, other factors believed to cause the condition include malnutrition and other diseases like thyroid disease, diabetes and increased appetite among other factors.

Diagnosing this health condition can be very involving. A vet will normally set out to ascertain whether the condition is a simple behavioral problem or a medical condition, in which case he/she will undertake a complete biochemistry profile, blood count and urine analysis. Treating this condition depends on causative factors. While a change of your Ocicat environment may help in case the causative factor is ascertained to behavioral, a vet may prescribe specific medications should the causative factor be medically related.

Urine Incontinence - This is a case of lack of control of the bladder, just in the same way it is in humans. Your Ocicat will present different symptoms if it has this health condition. Such include frequent urination, wet hair between its rear legs or on the abdomen, skin inflammation around its genitals and wet bedding among other symptoms.

There are simply many factors that can make your cat lose control of its bladder. Some of these include neutering/spaying procedures that disrupt the nerves around the bladder, lesions on the brain, overactive bladder syndrome, UTIs, lesions on the spinal cord and underdevelopment of the bladder among many other causes.

Diagnosing urine incontinence in cats can be very challenging because of the many possible causes. A vet will however strive to ascertain the particular cause before designing an effective treatment plan that may take some time. Treatment normally depends on the ascertained cause.

Mesothelioma - Mesothelioma refers to a rare type of tumour that develops on the cellular tissue lining the interior part of a cat's body, the epithelial linings. These linings play the important role of protecting the internal organs by covering them. They also facilitate movement within the body.

Just like with other types of tumour, Mesothelioma develops when mesothelial cells fail to divide or replicate in the normal way before migrating to other parts of the body, which further spreads the tumour.

Your Ocicat will show several symptoms if affected including difficulty in breathing, muffled lung/heart sounds, general body weakness, vomiting, inability to exercise and enlarged abdomen among other symptoms.

Diagnosing this condition normally involves a vet undertaking a complete blood profile, blood count and urinalysis. A vet may also obtain X-ray image of your Ocicat's abdomen/chest, radiography and ultrasound to observe the presence of masses in the body cavities. Drainage of unnecessary fluids within the body is usually the first line of treatment before medications are prescribed.

Stertor/Stridor - While Stertor refers to a cat's low-pitched, noisy breathing, Stridor refers to the high-pitched noisy breathing that your Ocicat can exhibit. Stertor is most likely to occur when your Ocicat inhales air. It is similar to snoring except that your cat's inhalation of air will be constricted, resulting in a low-pitched breathing occasioned by vibration of tissues that align the throat. On the other hand, Stridor is likely to occur when your cat inhales air with throat tissues in a rigid state.

Your cat will exhibit a number of symptoms when affected. These include inability to meow and extra-ordinary nature of breathing among other symptoms. These two related conditions can be caused by narrowed nostrils, inverted laryngeal, paralysis of the voice box/windpipe, tumour of the voice box and presence of foreign matter within the windpipe.

There are also risk factors associated with the occurrence of the two health conditions. Some of these include an environment with high temperatures, high metabolic rate, over-exercising and poor drinking/eating habits among other possible risk factors.

Diagnosis of the two conditions usually involves a vet obtaining your cat's health history, performing an internal imaging procedure (fluoroscopy) and X-ray imaging of the neck to identify any abnormalities in the neck's soft tissues. There are instances where a vet may need to perform surgery when foreign matter is lodged within the windpipe.

Baylisascarisis - This is what is referred to as Raccoon disease in cats. The disease also affects humans. It is transmitted by larvae of Baylisascarisis procyyonis parasite (roundworm) found in faeces left open in the environment. Your cat is most likely to contract the larvae if is used to venturing outdoors into areas with other cats having the parasite.

Your cat will present several symptoms if affected. These include un-coordinated walking, difficulty in swallowing, regular seizures and general confusion among other symptoms.

Diagnosis of this disease is through laboratory examination of faecal smear test that should detect presence of the disease in your cat's intestines. The larvae should be seen through ophthalmoscopic examination. There are a good number of medications that a vet can prescribe for your cat including Corticosteroids and albendazole medications.

Idiopathic Epilepsy - This is seizures in cats. It is a disorder that occurs in a cat's brain and causes sudden and in almost all cases uncontrolled/recurring attacks. If affected, your cat may or may not lose consciousness. Your cat will normally have a short aura and look as if it is under threat. It will eventually fall on its side at the onset of an attack and may salivate, defecate or urinate. An attack can last between 20 and 90 seconds before it recovers.

Seizures can occur when your cat is awake or when it is asleep. The period soon after an attack is usually followed by behaviour such as general confusion, blindness, increased thirst, increased appetite and aimless wondering among other abnormal behaviours.

The exact cause(s) of idiopathic epilepsy remains largely unknown, although it has been proved to be a hereditary health condition. Diagnosis of the condition normally involves blood cell count, thyroid screening and testing for viral infections if any. Treatment of this condition normally involves administration of anticonvulsant medications.

Constipation/Obstipation - Constipation is a condition where your Ocicat finds it hard to defecate. The condition is characterized by incomplete, infrequent and defecation difficulty. On the other hand, Obstipation refers to worsened constipation. It is pronounced constipation characterized by lack of bowel movement, in which case a cat does not defecate at all.

You can easily tell when your Ocicat has constipation. Apart from straining when defecating, it will also loose appetite. You may also notice swelling around the anus. Your Ocicat is also most likely to produce hard and dry faeces with very little amount of urine.

Defecation can be caused by various factors including swallowed hair, swallowed bones, excess fiber in your Ocicat's food, lack of exercise and low blood calcium among many other factors. It is very important that you do not allow constipation to develop further into Obstipation. It may be necessary to take your cat to a vet who will be able to undertake proper diagnosis of the cause.

Treating constipation depends on the cause. A vet may recommend dietary supplementation or rehydration. A vet may also undertake manual removal of faeces in the case of Obstipation. Surgery may be the only option in cases of serious Obstipation. It is very important that you regularly monitor your Ocicat's stool with the aim of detecting constipation in good time.

Hematoma/Seroma – Hematoma refers to a condition where blood collects in one spot outside blood vessels. On the other hand, Seroma refers to the same except that the collected blood does not contain any red blood cells; it is purely serum. Both hematoma and Seroma can occur in any part of your Ocicat's body including within the ears and brain. The most common happen to be sub-dermal hematoma/Seroma that develops just under the cat's skin.

The symptoms that hematoma/Seroma present depend on area of the body affected. Symptoms for sub-dermal hematoma/Seroma include swelling under the skin and itchiness around the area. Hematoma/Seroma that develops in the head or brain presents such symptoms as seizures and coma. Hematoma/Seroma can be caused by various factors including trauma and in some cases serious insect bites.

It is very important that you give your Ocicat a thorough physical examination when bathing. Doing so makes it possible to detect any unusual symptoms that may be of sub-dermal hematoma. A vet should be able to carry out physical and other tests on blood/serum drawn from the affected part for proper diagnosis. A vet can also perform imaging tests including X-ray, ultrasound, CT and MRI to diagnose internal hematoma/Seroma.

While minor hematoma/Seroma do re-absorb and resolve on their own without any medication, a vet is obligated to undertake treatment procedures to resolve serious cases. Treatment involves draining the collected blood/serum and surgery in case of internal hematoma/Seroma.

Accidents - Although all cats are susceptible to accidents, Ocicats stand the greatest risk of getting involved in accidents. This is simply because of their playful nature and the fact that they like heights. This is why it is very important that you make your home as cat friendly as possible by removing any sharp objects on the floor that they can fall on. Serious injuries require that you take your cat to a vet at the earliest possible time since it can be life-threatening.

Signs of Illness

Diseases do not develop overnight. It takes time before your cat finally falls ill. You need to be able to notice when your cat starts to show abnormal behaviour even before it falls ill. You can only do this having interacted and socialized with your cat to a point where you can easily tell when it is about to fall ill. Signs of illness in cats can be categorized into two types; behavioural and physical signs.

Behavioural Signs

You should be able to notice different, unusual behaviours by your cat, behaviours that should prompt you to take your cat to a vet at the earliest possible opportunity unless you know the reason for any unusual behaviour.

Although your cat will avoid its litter box when the box is unclean, avoidance is usually a clear sign of a medical condition. Urination outside the litter box can be a sign of medical conditions such as diabetes, urinary tract infection or kidney failure. You need to take your cat to a vet if you notice this unusual behaviour more than once when the litter box is perfectly clean.

Cats generally are not fond of drinking water. They obtain the water they need from their food. Although your cat will occasionally drink water, increased intake of water should be a cause of concern. This will be a sign of thirst, which is usually a sign of such health conditions/diseases as diabetes and hyperthyroidism among other diseases.

Failure by your cat to eat as it normally does should be a serious cause for concern. This may be an indication of loss of appetite that may in turn be a sign of many diseases including gingivitis, trauma or anemia among many other diseases.

Interacting and socializing with your cat should make it possible for you to know when and why it meows. Excess meowing (vocalization) may be a sign of stress, fear, sickness, pain or other medical conditions.

Your Ocicat is most likely to spend a better part of the day and in particular the morning hours sleeping. Although this is perfectly normal, excessive sleep in addition to hiding when it is awake should be a sign of fear, anxiety or sickness.
Being people-oriented, your Ocicat will most likely get into the habit of welcoming you whenever you arrive at home. You will need to be concerned with any change in this habit. You will need to establish where your cat goes when not welcoming you. It is most likely that you will find your cat in its litter box, which should alert you of a medical problem.

Physical Signs

Unlike behavioural signs of sickness, physical signs are easy to notice and one of the most obvious signs you should be able to notice is a change in your cat's coat appearance. The fact that cats generally groom themselves means that your cat's coat should always be smooth. You should be concerned when the coat appears ruffled, which may be a sign of malnutrition, parasitic infection or such other skin disorders as ringworm or allergy.

Your cat should always have good breath. Bad breath will definitely not be normal since such may be a sign of diabetes, gingivitis, kidney disease or gastrointestinal disorder among other diseases/health conditions.

Any rapid weight loss or gain should be a serious concern. This is because it may be a sign of many health conditions including malnutrition, overfeeding, diabetes, kidney failure or heart disease among many others.

When to Visit a Vet

Regardless of your Ocicat's age, five very important factors determine how healthy it will be; proper nutrition and weight management, environment, good dental care, parasite control and vaccinations. The food that you feed your cat determines whether or not it will remain healthy throughout its lifetime. You also need to make your cat's environment as friendly as possible to allow it to enjoy its life to the fullest. Ensure that you do not only socialize with your cat but engage in play activities as well.

Ensuring that your Ocicat's oral health is at its optimum will also go a long way in preventing many diseases. Closely related to environment is the issue of parasites. Note that parasites thrive in unhygienic locations and it is therefore very necessary to ensure that your cat's room or space remains clean all the time. Lastly, you need to ensure that your Ocicat receives all the recommended vaccinations and any other vaccination that may be fronted by relevant authorities from time to time.

When to take your cat to a vet depends on its age. Although kittens are in most cases sold off when they have already received the most important vaccinations, you will need to take yours to a vet at least three times a year for any additional vaccinations or routine checkups. Doing so will make it possible for you to know any health issues that your kitten may have once it comes of age.

An adult Ocicat does not require too much veterinary attention so long as you feed it on recommended foods and keep its environment clean. Your adult Ocicat will have received the recommended vaccinations and should be in a position to remain healthy for a long time. You will however need to take it to a vet at least twice a year for routine checkups.

Having an old or aging Ocicat can be a little of a problem because of the many visits you may need to make to a vet clinic. This is because it is during old age that age-related diseases/health conditions such as arthritis and heart disease among others set in. You will need to take your aging Ocicat to a vet at least three times in a year for routine medical checkups and for such indicated diseases/health conditions.

Your cat's general health remains squarely in your hands. You should take every step possible to ensure that your cat is not at risk of contracting any disease. You should be in a position to perform at-home physical examinations on a regular basis with the aim of determining your cat's general health condition.

Although you need to take your kitten, cat or aging cat to a vet as indicated, there are instances when it becomes necessary to take it to a vet at the earliest opportunity possible. Incidents such as accidents require that you take your Ocicat to a vet for immediate medical attention.

The Veterinarian

The professionals commonly referred to as veterinarians or vets in short are actually veterinary physicians trained to treat diseases, disorders and injuries that affect non-human animals. Vets are referred to differently in different countries around the world. Although they are generally referred to as vets, they are professionally referred to as veterinary surgeons in the UK for instance.

Different countries have strict legislations when it comes to veterinary services, just the same way it is with human physicians. It is mandatory in almost all countries for anyone using the term vet to have undertaken the necessary training, registered and licensed to practice as a vet. Vets work in many institutions. There are those who work in vet clinics where they engage with animal owners or pet owners directly in treating their livestock. There are also those who work in institutions like zoos, research institutions and animal hospitals.

Just in the same way that human doctors specialize in a specific area, vets also specialize. You are therefore most likely to come across a vet who is a surgery or dermatology specialist or one specializing in internal medicine. Generally however, vets diagnose and treat non-human diseases and health conditions in addition to providing aftercare and administration of vaccines.

It is common practice to find vets in different countries working in the private sector. Only a small number work in government institutions. The fact that the majority work in the private sectors and in particular in clinics allows them to work directly with animal owners; owners whose animals have varied diseases and health conditions.

The fact that you plan to buy or already own a cat and an Ocicat for that matter will obviously make it necessary to pay a vet a visit. This can be on the first day when you bring the cat home for the requisite vaccine(s). Just like with choosing your personal physician, you need to carefully choose a vet to engage for your cat's treatment and administration of vaccines.

How to Find a Good Vet

The fact that most vets work in clinics and private clinics makes finding the best vet a big challenge. This can be very true if you live in a location where there are many practicing vets. The first way to find the right vet is to enquire from close family members, neighbours and friends with pets. They should be able to refer you to a vet they personally know and who provides quality service.

Apart from making enquiries, you also have the option of consulting your local professional organization for information on licensed vets practicing in your locality. You also have the option of getting information on the right vets from a local cat breeder. A breeder in particular will be better placed to refer you to the right vet because he/she obviously engages the service of a vet to treat his/her cats in the cattery.

Whether you choose to make enquiries or contact a professional organization or a cat breeder, there are certainly several issues you will need to ascertain before you engage the service of a vet and one of these issues is whether or not the vet is licensed and has some accreditation. A professional and ethical vet will normally share with you his/her certification, which should ideally be posted on the office wall. You will also need to ascertain whether or not the vet is a member of a local professional organization.

Apart from a vet's certification, accreditation and level of experience, you need to undertake an overall assessment of the facility with knowledge that it is at that clinic where you will henceforth be bringing your Ocicat in case of health problems. It is therefore important to assess a facility's level of cleanliness among other issues.

It is common for vets to enter into agreements with pet owners for the purpose of taking care of their pets' health. Although most pet owners are in favour of such agreements as one way of cutting down on their pets' health care costs, doing so can be costly without due diligence.

It is possible that you and your pet's vet can have disagreements that force you to engage the service of a different vet. Terminating an agreement can be very costly depending on the agreement period you agreed upon. The best way to cutting down on your Ocicat's health care costs is to shop for a suitable pet insurance policy that covers risks that your cat is susceptible to.

Cat Insurance

Your Ocicat is not only people friendly; it turns out to be the best companion you can have at home as a pet. Furthermore, it makes you active because of its playful nature. It is definitely a valuable family member. Just in the same way that you ensure your other family members are comfortable and in good health, you need to ensure that your cat also remains in good health and one way to go about this is to take out cat insurance for your Ocicat.

It is a fact that veterinary fees and medication costs are always on the rise, which can make it impossible for you to meet your cat's medical costs at a time it needs it most. Taking out an appropriate cat insurance policy goes a long way in keeping your veterinary costs low while giving your cat good health care.

Regardless of your location, any cat insurance policy you are likely to find is designed to cover the cost of veterinary fees and treatment of diseases/health conditions and injuries. Although very important, choosing the right cat insurance policy for your Ocicat can be a big challenge. This is because there are simply many policies out there on the market that differ in terms of what they cover and price. This makes it necessary to know the best time to take out cat insurance.

The best time to take out cat insurance is when your cat is a kitten. This is because age is one of the most important factors pet insurance companies take into consideration when determining the level of insurance premium to quote. Kittens generally attract low premium rates compared to adult and aging cats that attract high premium rates because of various factors including the onset of age-related diseases/health conditions.

There are generally four types of cat insurance policies you can choose from; lifetime, maximum benefit, limited time and accident-only policies.

Lifetime cat insurance policy covers vet fees for one year. You will need to continuously renew the policy to enjoy the same cover at the same premium rate regardless of how many claims you make. Although the cost of this policy is usually on the higher side, it is beneficial taking into account the fact that your cat remains covered for its lifetime even when it develops a life-long disease.

Unlike the lifetime policy, the maximum benefit policy provides cover for a pre-determined maximum amount of veterinary fees per health condition. The specific health condition is considered a pre-existing condition and is therefore excluded from future claims once the maximum limit is reached.

The time limited policy is similar to the maximum benefit policy except that the latter is limited to one year only, a period in which vet fees can be offset for each health condition.

The accident-only policy is limited to treatment of injuries your Ocicat may sustain from accidents at home or outside the home including on the road.

A common feature of almost all cat insurance policies is the exclusion of pre-existing medical conditions. Other procedures such as preventative treatments, pregnancy/birth, neutering/spaying and worm control are also excluded from the policies. It is very important that you undertake a little research with the aim of finding a pet insurance company that quotes low premium rates on policies that provide a specific cover you need for your Ocicat.

Chapter 11 – Vaccinations

What is a Vaccine?

A vaccine is basically a solution containing antigens that to the body's immune system looks like a disease-causing organism, but is not. Your Ocicat can be given a vaccine orally or through injection. When introduced into the body, the vaccine stimulates the body's complex immune system, making the system strong enough to fight any disease-causing organism that enters the body. Having your cat vaccinated is therefore very important.

Different jurisdictions have different vaccine requirements for all pets including cats. While some vaccines are only available in particular regions of the world because of the prevalence of specific cat diseases, others are only available in other regions. There are basically two types of vaccines; core and non-core vaccines. While core vaccines are mandatory to all cats regardless of region or location, non-core vaccines are only found in specific regions or locations.

Like with anything introduced into the body, vaccines present several symptoms including fever, vomiting, loss of appetite, sluggishness, diarrhoea and swelling around injection area. There are also serious symptoms that may occur depending on the kind of vaccine your cat receives. These include life-threatening allergic reactions and the development of a tumour around the injected area. The serious symptoms are however limited in occurrence. Vaccine symptoms are generally mild and do fade away within a few days.

Safety of Vaccines

Although cat vaccines are generally safe, there has been controversy around some vaccines that are often considered unnecessary. You need to appreciate the fact that it is because of feline vaccines that cats can now live beyond their expected life-span. The production and administration of most vaccines that had raised controversies have luckily ceased. It is therefore perfectly safe to take your Ocicat to a vet to receive the core vaccines. In any case, you are most likely to buy an Ocicat kitten already vaccinated.

One major challenge that many cat owners face is when to have their cats vaccinated. There are different circumstances and instances when your Ocicat needs to be vaccinated.

Kitten Vaccination

Your Ocicat kitten or cat is most likely to have received its first vaccination while still with the breeder you bought it from. Even so, the vaccination must have been several weeks after it was born. This is because kittens naturally acquire sufficient immunity from their mothers through milk. Furthermore, a kitten's immune system is still not yet fully developed to receive artificial vaccinations.

Breeders do arrange with veterinarians for their kittens to be vaccinated once they attain the age of seven weeks with additional vaccinations administered when they are twelve and again once they attain the age of sixteen years. The two additional vaccinations are in most cases boosters that fortify the first vaccination.

Adult Cat Immunization

Adult cats are not vaccinated but rather immunized. Like with vaccination, immunization is aimed at further boosting your Ocicat's immune system to continue being effective in offering protection against possible infections.

Core Cat Vaccines

Core cat vaccines are those that all cats should receive regardless of location. These vaccines are very effective in offering protection against life-threatening diseases found in all regions of the world. They include:

Feline Viral Rhinotracheitis (FVR) Vaccine
FVR Vaccine is administered to protect against the FVR virus that is at times referred to as feline influenza or feline pneumonia. This is a respiratory disease found across the globe.

FVR is a highly contagious disease that can kill kittens within a few days of infection. The disease is easily transmitted through direct contact. One cat passes the disease on to another cat through saliva, nasal and eye secretions. When infected, your cat will most likely show signs like coughing, sneezing, excessive nasal discharge, loss of appetite and high fever.

Feline Calicivirus (FCV) Vaccine
Your cat receives this vaccination to protect itself against the virus that causes respiratory infection. Occurrence of this disease usually ends in an epidemic in areas with a large cat population because of its highly contagious nature.

FCV presents symptoms such as nose/eye discharge, mouth ulceration, anorexia and general body weakness at the initial stage. If affected, your Ocicat is most likely to present such secondary symptoms as jaundice, high fever, swelling of the face and limbs (oedema) and dysfunction of organs within the body.

Feline Panleukopenia Virus (FPV) Vaccine
The FPV vaccine is one of the most important cat vaccines that your cat must receive. This is because the vaccine offers protection against the highly contagious and fatal diseases caused by the Panleukopenia virus that causes low white blood cells. The disease is largely transmitted through contact with the bodily fluids of an infected cat.

If infected, your Ocicat is most likely to show signs of severe dehydration, bloody diarrhoea, anemia, depression, vomiting, loss of appetite, self-biting and loss of skin elasticity among other signs. Pregnant cats affected by the disease give birth to kittens with cerebellar hypopasia.

117

Feline Immunodeficiency Virus (FIV) Vaccine

FIV is often referred to as feline AIDS. This is so because it is in many ways similar to the human immunodeficiency virus (HIV). There are different types of FIV that the FIV Vaccine is designed to protect against. Like in humans, your Ocicat is most likely to live with FIV in case of infection, in which case it will now be a carrier of the virus.

FIV attacks the immune system just in the same way that HIV does in humans. Although FIV and HIV are similar, humans cannot contract FIV and cats cannot contract HIV. Should your cat be infected, it will henceforth transmit the virus to other cats through saliva. Outdoor cats happen to be more at risk of contracting the FIV virus compared to indoor cats.

Non-Core Cat Vaccines

Although classified as non-core cat vaccines, vaccines in this category are core in some regions of the world. This is because they are designed to offer cats protection against specific diseases only found in certain regions. They include:

Feline Leukaemia Virus (FLV) Vaccine

FLV is a virus that causes life-threatening diseases in cats. One common disease associated with the virus is leukaemia, which develops when the virus destroys blood cells, in effect making them cancerous. The virus presents several symptoms including loss of appetite, poor coat condition, skin infections, fatigue, oral infections including gingivitis, diarrhoea and jaundice among many other symptoms. Your Ocicat, if infected, will be able to transmit the virus to other cats through saliva, litter box (sharing) and food/water dishes.

Rabies Vaccine

Rabies was in the past a universal medical condition that affected humans, dogs and other warm-blooded animals such as cats. Vaccination campaigns undertaken in specific regions of the world made it possible for the disease to be eradicated in such regions. The rabies vaccine is now only common in specific regions where cats, dogs and humans are still vulnerable to Rabies infections.

Rabies is a serious disease that you should protect your Ocicat from by ensuring that it receives the necessary vaccination. It is a viral disease that causes serious inflammation of the brain. It presents such symptoms as fever, loss of consciousness and restricted movement among other symptoms. Most rabies cases result in death.

Chlamydophila Felis Vaccine

Chlamydophila felis is a bacteria commonly found in cats. The vaccine for the bacteria is designed to protect against it. The bacteria cause inflammation of a cat's conjunctiva, rhinitis and respiratory health problems.

Depending on your location, you may be required from time to time to take your cat to a local vet for specific vaccinations aimed at preventing identified cat diseases in your specific area. Such vaccinations are in most cases occasioned by an outbreak of cat diseases. Different countries have legislations that make such vaccinations mandatory and failure to adhere to this subjects you to different penalties.

Apart from being a requirement of legislation, you need to consider your cat's vaccination seriously. This is because you are the ultimate beneficiary knowing that your cat is fully vaccinated or immunized and therefore well protected from diseases that can affect its health. It is therefore very important that you consult your local vet on a regular basis for proper information on cat vaccinations and immunizations.

Chapter 12 – Costs

Estimated Monthly/Yearly Maintenance Costs

Owning an Ocicat is simply fulfilling. Not only is it a pet but a valuable companion as well. However, being responsible for your lovely Ocicat comes at a cost, which you are obligated to bear. Although maintaining a cat can be very expensive, you can keep maintenance costs low so long as you stick to feeding it an appropriate diet, ensuring that it receives all the necessary vaccinations/immunizations and maintaining proper hygiene at home.

You should be capable of maintaining your Ocicat to make it different from any other Ocicat or other cats on the street. Failure to meet some of your Ocicat's needs and demands can easily be a cause of health problems. Furthermore, you stand the risk of losing your cat since it may simply run away onto the street.

There are different costs you are bound to incur when you plan to own and maintain an Ocicat. You are most likely to incur heavy expenses when you prepare to buy or adopt an Ocicat. Most of the costs relate to supplies that the cat will need soon after arriving at home. They include:

Food – There is no doubt that your cat will need to eat not just any food but good quality cat food. This will be an incurring expense. The cost of quality cat food averages at $120 - $150 (£71- £89) per month depending on your location. Yearly maintenance costs on food will therefore be around $1,800 (£ 1,072) in any given year.

Nutrition Supplements – These are dietary supplements that you may need to buy for your Ocicat. You will however need to consult a vet before buying any. Ideally, it is a vet who should inform you when your cat needs supplements, which may be because of a special need. You may need to incur about $100 (£60) at any given time on dietary supplements.

Food/Water Bowls – These are supplies you will need to buy before you bring your Ocicat home. Note that sharing of food/water bowls used by your cat will not be allowed. For instance, you should not feed your dog on the same food/water bowls used by your cat. Quality food/water bowls retail at around $10 - $30 (£6 - £18) depending on your location. Note that you may need to replace them at least twice in any given year, which makes yearly costs on food/water bowls between $60 - $90 (£35-£54).

Treats – Treats are edible food stuffs that you will need to feed your Ocicat once in a while. They are actually niceties that you use as rewards when your cat does something positive. You are most likely to offer your Ocicat treats more often during the first few months as you subject it to training, in which case you are bound to incur between $30 and $100 (£18 - £60) per month. Yearly treat costs average between $60 and $300 (£35- £178).

Grooming Supplies – Like with all cats, your Ocicat is naturally a clean cat that goes the extra mile to keep itself as clean as possible. It will therefore groom itself often to achieve this. You will still need to groom your cat, in which case you will be obligated to invest in quality grooming supplies. While you are bound to spend around $50 - $100 (£30 - £60) in buying permanent grooming supplies such as tools, you will spend between $30 - $60 (£18 - £35) on such other recurrent supplies as shampoos and odour removers every month. Your Ocicat's yearly grooming costs will average between $200 and $500 (£120 - £300).

Cat Bed – Your Ocicat will need a good place to sleep in and investing in a quality cat bed is highly recommended. A cat bed lasts a long time and you may only need to replace it when it is

121

very necessary. A good quality cat bed retails at between $20 and $100 (£12 - £60) depending on your location.

Cat Carrier – Like human babies, you will need to invest in a quality cat carrier for use in transporting your Ocicat. Cats are generally not fond of travelling in cars and having a carrier makes travelling with your cat trouble-free. A quality cat carrier will set you back financially by between $20 and $100 (£12 - £60). You may only need to replace it after two or three years.

Cat Toys – Your Ocicat is a playful and very active pet. This is why investing in quality cat toys is not only highly recommended but also very necessary. Having toys around will not only engage your cat in play but will also go a long way in helping it to release a lot of energy, energy that if it did not use would make living with your cat a little bit of a problem. Good quality cat toys retail at between $20 and $50 (£12 - £30) a piece and since you will need to buy different types, you should be ready to spend anything between $100 and $250 (£60 - £150) on toys once in a long time.

Scratching Post – Having a cat at home presents the risk of having your furniture scratched. This is because cats have a natural scratching instinct. The best way of dealing with the risk of having your furniture scratched is providing your cat with a scratching post, which costs between $50 and $100 (£30 - £60 only once.

Proper care of your Ocicat is not limited to making food and the other supplies available. You also need to ensure that your cat is in good health. Veterinary service will therefore be very necessary, at a cost. There are different veterinary services your Ocicat requires. They include:

Routine vet exams – These are routine vet exams a vet undertakes with the aim of determining your Ocicat's health condition. This can be three times a year for a kitten, twice for an adult cat and thrice for an aging cat. You will be obligated to incur between $50 and $200 (£30 - £120) for such exams in any given year depending on your cat's age.

Vaccinations/Immunizations – Although you are most likely to adopt or buy a vaccinated Ocicat, there are immunizations it will need to receive once it comes of age. Such immunizations cost between $50 and $150 (£30 - £90) per year.

Spaying/Neutering – You may choose to have your Ocicat spayed/neutered, in which case it will not be able to bring forth offspring. Having your cat spayed/neutered will cost you between $150 and $300 (£89 - £180), a one-off expense.

Emergency Care – You certainly will not rule out your Ocicat getting injured, which will require emergency veterinary care. Depending on the nature of injury and your location, you are most likely to incur between $500 and $2,000 (£300 - £1,190) on emergency care, which may involve surgery.

Veterinary costs can be huge to the extent that they exceed any other cat maintenance expenses. This is why many cat owners choose to buy cat insurance policies that cover risks that their cats are exposed to, something which you too may consider.

Maintaining your Ocicat requires that you be ready to commit yourself financially for its overall well-being and health. On average, your Ocicat's monthly maintenance cost will range between $400 and $700 (£238 - £416) and around $1,500 - $5,000 (£890- £2980) yearly.

Maintaining a cat can indeed be a very expensive undertaking. There are, however, several ways through which you can cut down on maintenance expenses and one of these is buying cat food in bulk. You can cut cat food expenses by almost 50% by simply buying the same in bulk. The best way to do this is to buy at wholesale price, which guarantees you an attractive discount. Apart from cat food, cat treatment is the other recurrent expenditure you are most likely to incur throughout your cat's life. Taking your cat to the vet whenever it falls sick or when it gets injured and paying out of pocket can be very expensive. You need to consider taking out the best cat insurance for your cat. It will be appropriate to shop for a cat insurance policy that covers most of the diseases and health conditions that your cat is susceptible to.

It is not mandatory to buy your cat's equipment including toys. You can effectively make use of locally available materials to make equipment such as a scratch post, cat bed, cat tree and food/water dishes. You can make these as DIY projects or engage the service of a local artist to make them for you at a very minimal cost.

Chapter 13 – Care For Your Aging Ocicat

Major milestones have been achieved in the last decade or so when it comes to the treatment of cat diseases and management of cat health conditions. Improvements of existing cat medications and the discovery of new cat treatment methods has made it possible for cats to live much longer than their expected lifespan.

Although all cats of all ages benefit from such improvements, aging cats are the biggest beneficiaries. This is because properly cared for aging cats can now age gracefully without necessarily experiencing the pain and a lot of discomfort that aging cats hitherto experienced in the past.

Although your Ocicat generally has a lifespan of 15 years, it can live to attain the age of 18 years so long as you provide it with proper care including veterinary care.

What is aging?
Aging is a process that every living being goes through. It is a natural process that sets in when life expectancy is attained, which in this case is 15 years for Ocicats. One day in a cat's life is a very long time taking into account the fact that a year in a cat's life is similar to about 15 years for humans. Likewise, a cat aged 15 is like a human being 85 years. Just like in humans, the onset of aging in cats brings with it several challenges, some which can make your Ocicat very uncomfortable if you do not offer the necessary help.

Physiological & Behavioural Changes
Your Ocicat will exhibit many changes once it attains old age. One of the most visible changes is the tendency to walk on its hocks. This is because its hind leg muscles become weak to a

point where running and jumping becomes difficult. This is the time to change its bed to a larger one because it finds it difficult to curl up in a small bed.

Your aging cat will also be very forgetful. It may choose to remain outdoors if it ventures out regardless of the weather. This is also the time when it can easily get lost if it is used to venturing out without company.

A visible sign of aging in cats is usually what is referred to as winding down. This is when it grows thinner, with its hip, shoulder and backbones becoming visible. In addition to becoming thinner, the fat layer just under the skin also melts away, further exposing the bones. It is important at this stage to consult a vet for advice on special types of cat food and dietary supplements to feed your cat.

The aging process also causes many faculty changes in a cat's life. Its hearing and cognition abilities diminish to a great extent. Furthermore, its metabolic rate also decreases. If Ocicat is not used to venturing outdoors, it is bound to feel cold most of the time. It is your responsibility to ensure that your cat sleeps in warm bedding in addition to taking it out to receive sunshine when it is possible.

One fact you need to remember when your Ocicat ages is that its immunity reduces, making it highly susceptible to many infections. It becomes very necessary to take your cat to a vet whenever you notice any strange behaviour or symptoms for immediate care.

Although Ocicats are generally people-oriented pets, your aging Ocicat will be more attention-seeking than at any other time. This is because it naturally knows that it is incapacitated in many ways and will want to be near you most of the time for comfort, assurance and help. Your cat will tend to sleep for much longer.

126

Because of the many behavioural and physiological changes that your Ocicat is bound to go through once the aging process sets in, it is most likely to engage less in physical activities. It is however very important that you exercise your cat's mind. Limited physical exercise is also necessary to help your cat overcome any discomfort it may experience because of diseases like arthritis, which aging cats are highly susceptible to.

Health Challenges in Old Cats

Your aging Ocicat experiences a lot of changes including reduced immunity. This exposes it to many diseases/health conditions that you must take note of with the aim of helping it cope. Some of the health challenges your cat is most likely to face include:

Parasite Infestation

Your aging Ocicat will probably not groom itself as it used to do. This exposes it to a parasite infestation and in particular ticks and fleas. This will likely happen if it is used to going outdoors. Infestation of these parasites will easily lead to skin infections. The likelihood of your cat becoming anemic also becomes high. This is when it becomes necessary to use flea spray or powder. Although you have the alternative of using flea collars, they have the disadvantage of being ineffective. Furthermore, flea collars can also cause an allergic reaction. Your Ocicat is also likely to have internal parasites if it is used to going outdoors, just in the same way it used to do when it was a kitten. It becomes necessary for your aging cat to receive treatment for worms and in particular roundworms after every three months.

Blindness

In addition to health challenges such as hearing loss and loss of memory, a major challenge that your aging Ocicat is likely to face is blindness. This starts as partial loss of vision before developing into total blindness.

Although you may not be able to know when your cat is losing its vision, there are specific signs you need to look out for. These include reluctance to move, misjudging heights, clumsiness, eye rubbing, large pupils and when it easily gets startled. Because treating blindness due to old age is simply impossible, the best you can do to help your Ocicat cope is ensure that it moves in a secure environment, offer help all the time and speak to it often.

Pain
Diseases/health conditions such as arthritis that your aging Ocicat is susceptible to are usually accompanied by pain. Your cat may tremble, shiver or crouch. It becomes very important to understand your cat's body language with the aim of offering help. It becomes necessary to take your cat to a vet for proper diagnosis of the existing disease and for appropriate pain medications.

Dental Infections
Old cats are highly susceptible to dental infections. About 70% of all old cats suffer from dental infections mostly caused by the formation of plaque. It is during your cat's old age that you must ensure that it receives regular dental care that involves the removal of plaque that forms tartar, which in effect leads to gingivitis.

Arthritis
Arthritis is the most common health problem that cats in old age suffer from, just like in humans. This health condition is usually accompanied by joint pain; pain that can make your cat very uncomfortable. Your cat will find it very difficult to engage in physical activities. The best way to help your cat cope is to consult a local vet for the best supplements to buy (supplements that support the rebuilding of joint cartilage).

Reduced Heart Function
Just like in humans, your cat's heart function reduces once old age sets in. Its heart muscles do not only weaken but also enlarge. It becomes necessary to take your cat to a vet for regular checkups and to give medications that strengthen the heart muscles.

Chapter 14 – What To Do with an Old Ocicat

Living with an old cat or an old Ocicat for that matter can be a serious challenge, especially if it becomes senile. You simply will not cope with the amount of care it needs to continue living comfortably. It is because of this that you may look for alternative ways of how your Ocicat can still receive proper care until it dies. You have three options:

Cat Rescue Centre

Taking your aged Ocicat to a dedicated cat rescue centre may be your only option of letting your aged cat go. Although it can be very difficult, doing so will lessen your burden of having to watch over it all the time.

Cat rescue centers are institutions established by organizations like animal welfare societies. Such centers are usually staffed with qualified pet personnel with the necessary skills on taking care of pets of all ages. In addition to admitting aged pets, including cats at a small fee, they also offer younger pets for adoption.

Most cat rescue centers are funded by donations received from pet lovers and other organizations. Some well established cat rescue centers serve as educational institutions where pet lovers have the opportunity to learn more about pets they are interested in buying or adopting.

Taking your old Ocicat to a cat rescue centre does not in any way mean disposing of it. Most rescue centers allow owners to visit their aged cats, a good opportunity to reconnect with pets they have lived with for a long time.

Euthanasia

Euthanasia is the other route or option you have when it comes to dealing with your old Ocicat. Most cat owners whose cats are aged choose to have their cats euthanized instead of taking them to cat rescue centers. The main reason for this is the fact that having their cats euthanized eliminates the worry they would otherwise continuously have over their pets at such centers.

Simply put, euthanasia is the practice whereby life is ended. You may choose to have your aged Ocicat euthanized in order to relieve it from the pain, anguish, suffering and discomfort it goes through as it waits for its natural death. Different jurisdictions have different laws relating to euthanasia for humans and pets. Your vet should be in a good position to enlighten you on what laws apply in your jurisdiction.

Just like in the case of humans, a vet will normally require that you sign a consent form before euthanizing your cat. The signing of the form absolves a vet from any claim you make thereafter that he/she caused your cat's death. There are however certain instances where vets request pet owners for permission to euthanize their aged pets. Such cases are usually when vets discover serious diseases in the cause of treating cats. Even in such situations, cat owners have the last word on whether or not their cats should be euthanized.

Whether you take your cat to a vet clinic to be euthanized or call a vet to undertake the procedure at home, the procedure is the same. The procedure normally involves giving an over-dose of anesthesia into the main vein in one of its forelegs. In the case of difficult or troublesome cats, a crush cage is normally used.

The injection of anesthesia leads to immediate unconsciousness followed by a slow death. Your Ocicat is most likely to exhale and pass urine as body muscles relax after death. To ensure that your cat is indeed dead, a vet may give an additional injection of anesthesia into the kidney or the heart. Your lovely Ocicat will most likely die with its eyes open and a vet will simply close the eyes before placing the cat in a position where it appears to be just asleep. It is only after this that a vet wraps your cat in a black bag both for safety and privacy before handing it over to you.

Watching your Ocicat die can be a very traumatizing experience. The experience can remain in your mind for a very long time. This is why some cat owners choose to remain in a separate room when a vet undertakes euthanasia on their aged cats and other pets.

Most cat owners choose to call a vet to perform the procedure in their homes rather than at a vet's clinic, a move that you too may consider. This is because having the procedure undertaken at home is somehow less traumatic.

The cost of euthanasia varies from one region to another and from one vet to another. The cost can actually be on the higher side if you choose to call a vet to undertake the procedure at home. Generally, the cost ranges between $30 and $60 (£17- £35) across the world. It is always recommended that you settle any outstanding amount with a vet before he/she undertakes the procedure. This is because you may not find it comfortable talking about payments when your cat is already dead.

Home Care

You may choose not to take your aged Ocicat to a cat rescue centre or have it euthanized. You may take this route if you are fond of your cat and have the time to provide it with all the necessary care it needs until it dies a natural death. Although most cat owners choose to care for their cats at home until they die, the suffering, pain and anguish they go through can similarly be traumatizing.

Body Disposal

Taking your aged Ocicat to a cat rescue centre may eliminate your responsibility to dispose of the body when it finally dies. This will depend on the agreement between you and a care centre management. Most centers do undertake to dispose of bodies of dead cats. Depending on your arrangement, you may be informed. Having your cat euthanized at a vet's clinic, at home or if you choose to care for your cat at home, you will have to determine how to dispose of the body.

Burial

The burial of pets is fast becoming popular around the world and it is highly possible that you too may choose to bury your Ocicat when it dies. Even so, you need to acquaint yourself with your local by-laws that relate to the disposal of dead pet bodies. You will need to bury your cat soon enough before it putrefies unless you have a freezer where you can store the body for a few days. You may choose to bury your cat in your back garden or at your local authority's pet cemetery.

Even so, there are instances when you may not be allowed to bury your cat. Such are instances where the body poses a degree of risk to human health. This may apply if your cat dies of rabies in which case it will be the responsibility of a vet to dispose of the body.

Cremation

Like with burial, cremation is another popular way of disposing of dead bodies. You may choose to have the body of your Ocicat cremated to give you the opportunity to bring its ashes home in a jar to scatter in its room/space or simply keep. It is common to find pet cemeteries having pet cremation facilities where you can have your cat cremated.

Taxidermy

You may choose to have your Ocicat taxidermized to at least allow you have it at home although in a static state. Taxidermy is a process where a professional taxidermist removes all the cat's internal organs including tissue and bones. The remaining skin is then stuffed to make your dead Ocicat look real.

Desiccation

At times referred to as freeze-drying, desiccation is the process where water is removed from your Ocicat's body. Your cat will simply be put in the right posture before being desiccated. The process can take as long as six months and most cat owners do like the result because of its lifelike nature. Because of environmental factors, the desiccated body is usually housed in a glass container for preservation. This gives you the opportunity to have your Ocicat at home even though dead.

Resin Preservation

This is another way you may choose to dispose off your dead Ocicat's body. It involves the removal of blood and other bodily fluids, which are replaced with resin. Resin has the characteristic of setting in solid, which in effect yields a lifelike body.

Post-Disposal Period

The period soon after disposing off your Ocicat's body can be a very trying time. It can indeed by a trying time if you have Ocicats and other pets at home. Do cats have feelings? Will they realize that one of them is missing? How will they cope knowing that one of them is missing? It is a fact that cats have feelings. Ocicats in particular develop a strong bond between them and will therefore be troubled by the absence of one of their own.

One thing you may notice when you have two Ocicats as pets is that each of them marks its own territory. One of them naturally becomes the leader of the other. The absence of one of them therefore traumatizes the remaining one. It may take some time before the remaining one adjusts. The best way to comfort the remaining one is to always give it as much attention as possible.

The situation can be very complicated to handle if you have children. This is because Ocicats get along very well with children because of their playful nature. Your dead cat will not have just been your kids' companion but a valuable playmate. They are bound to take its death very hard. The best you can do in such a situation is to make your kids understand what death is and why their playmate has died.

Making your kids understand what death is and that it applies to human beings can be very beneficial to them. This is because kids learn through experiences and knowing about death will make them appreciate the fact that death is natural and can happen to any family member at any time.

How to Cope with Your Ocicat's Death

Your Ocicat's death can be similar to the death of a child or a young family member. Knowing that you adopted or bought it, natured it to maturity and was a valuable companion that is no more can take a toll on your mind. Not only will you develop the feeling of loss but you will grieve for your cat. You will probably go into a state of denial, develop anger and mourn before accepting that your lovely Ocicat is no more. This may be the appropriate time to share your feelings with other family members. Doing so will no doubt go a long way in overcoming your anger and feeling of loss you may develop.

One reason why many cat owners choose to dispose off bodies of their cats is to have the opportunity to remember their cats knowing that it is buried in their backyards. Remembrance provides you and your family with a good opportunity to reflect back on the good times you had with your dead cat.

134

Replacing Your Dead Ocicat

Having lived with an Ocicat that is no more will most likely drive you to adopt or buy another to replace the dead one. When to have another one will however depend on several factors. One of the most important factors that may make it necessary to have another Ocicat soon after the death of the previous one is if you had two of them.

The loneliness that the remaining one will feel may make it necessary to get another one for company. You may also need to get another one soon after in case you have children. The other reason why you may need to replace your dead cat quickly relates to why you bought or adopted the dead one in the first place. You may simply like pets and Ocicats in particular. You may also be used to having a pet as a companion and cannot do without one.

Chapter 15 – Becoming an Ocicat Breeder

Who Is A Breeder?

With its beautiful short fur, clear eyes, perfect disposition, high intelligent and lovely spotted coat, you may choose to become an Ocicat breeder. The Ocicat breed is indeed a very popular breed in the world and becoming a breeder can assure you of a ready market, depending on your location.

A breeder is someone who is engaged in the business of mating carefully selected animals or plants to reproduce offspring that exhibit specific qualities and characteristics unique to a breed. Becoming an Ocicat breeder therefore involves breeding pre-bred Ocicats with the aim of reproducing kittens that exhibit the qualities and characteristics unique to the Ocicat breed.

You can become a breeder purely for fun, as a hobby or as a business. Whether you choose to breed Ocicats as a hobby or as a business, you will have a good opportunity to participate in professional cat shows and competitions. Becoming a breeder does not require that you must have attained a specific level of education. You must, however, demonstrate that you have compassion and a genuine interest in the Ocicat breed.

Things to Note

Although you may have compassion and interest in the Ocicat breed to a point where you want to become a breeder, there are important things you need to take note of. From the onset, becoming an Ocicat breeder will not make you rich overnight. Becoming a breeder can be very expensive and you should not expect to recoup your expenses in a short period. You need to start breeding as a hobby before you can expect to start receiving some income. Indeed, most current successful Ocicat breeders started off breeding as a hobby before graduating to full time commercial breeders.

The second thing to note is that the practice of breeding requires commitment, devotion and time. Time in particular is very important. It becomes very necessary that you devote most of your time to your cattery. This is because the cattery requires daily cleaning, feeding, grooming and treatment of your cats. This is the only way you will be able to breed healthy Ocicats that will encourage many in your neighbourhood to buy.

Thirdly, becoming an Ocicat breeder requires some level of financial investment. You will need to construct a cattery at a suitable location, install the necessary infrastructure, buy cat food and engage the service of a vet among other costs. You will also need to incur other expenses in having your cats registered by relevant bodies and pay some fee to your local authority. Most current Ocicat breeders stated off with only two cats in small rooms right within their homes, something that you too may consider.

Lastly, you need to be prepared to handle the emotional toll that comes along with the practice of breeding. The fact that you will be taking care of many cats and mating them means that they will be giving birth. It is common for some pregnant cats to die when giving birth in catteries. Others will die of natural causes including diseases. Kittens will also be at risk of dying of natural causes. Watching as your lovely Ocicats and kittens die will take a serious toll on your mind.

Where to Start

The best way to start off as a breeder is to prepare a room in your homestead to serve as your cattery on a temporary basis. This is not only cost effective; it will also be easy to manage your cats. Such preparation involves equipping the room with all the necessary equipment and supplies your cats will need to survive. These include food, water/food dishes, scratch post, bed and beddings and cat play toys among other equipment and supplies. You also need to engage the service of a veterinarian who will be responsible for treating your cats whenever they fall sick or get injured and in giving vaccinations.

The second step to becoming an Ocicat breeder is identifying an established breeder to buy Ocicat kittens or cats from. It is mandatory that you buy from an established and registered breeder. This is because such a breeder will be breeding pedigree Ocicats that are properly registered.

You have the option of buying a female Ocicat (queens), in which case you will be obligated to buy a male (tom) afterwards or take your Ocicat queen to a vet or breeder for insemination. You also have the option of buying two Ocicats; a tom and a queen. Depending on your preference and level of preparedness in becoming an Ocicat breeder, you may choose to buy kittens or adult cats.

The fourth step in becoming a breeder is to register as a breeder. You have several options on how to register, depending on your location and preference. There are both national and international cat registries from which you can choose one to register with. International cat registries include the UK's Cat Fanciers Association (CFA), France's Federation Internationale Feline (FIFe), UAE's Emirates Feline Federation (EFF), The American Cat Fanciers Association (ACFA) and The International Cat Association (TICA). National cat registries include the UK's Governing Council of the Cat Fancy (GCCF), the UK's Felis Britannica (member of FIFe), PRC's Cat Aficionado Association (CAA) and the Canadian Cat Association (CCA) among other national registries.

Registering your cats provides for several benefits. Firstly, you will be recognized as a registered breeder licensed to breed Ocicats. Secondly, you will have the opportunity to participate in both national and international cat shows and have your cats participate in different championships depending on their age. Participation in such championships can earn you good money depending on how your cats perform.

Thirdly, you will have the opportunity to learn better breeding techniques both from a registry you register with and other Ocicat breeders. Registering as a breeder also gives you the opportunity to know the exact breed standards you will have to maintain as an Ocicat breeder. Lastly, you will have the opportunity to be appointed as an Ocicat show judge after gaining reasonable breeding experience and if you so wish. Note that you can register with more than one registry if you so wish so long as you are financially capable of meeting all registration cost.

Different cat registries organize different Ocicat shows and competitions. CFA for example organizes the Kitten Shows and Championships (for pedigreed kittens aged between four and eight months), Championships (for unaltered cats aged eight months), Premiership (for altered cats aged eight months), Veteran (for both altered and unaltered cats aged seven years) and Household (for non-pedigreed cats aged four months).

Successful registration as an Ocicat breeder is just the first step to becoming a professional breeder. Because the cats you buy will have been registered by their breeder, you will need to register the litter that your cats give birth to. This you will do with a registry you registered with. Registering your litter entitles you to a unique prefix that will henceforth be used as the first name for all litter that your cats will produce. It will be your responsibility to indicate a prefix you will wish to use.

Different cat registries have different requirements when registering prefixes. The GCCF for example requires that you must have been registered as a breeder for at least one year before you can register your litter.

General Breeding Information

Unlike other cat breeds, Ocicats do become sexually active at a young age. Both your tom and queen become sexually active, with the queen capable of attaining pregnancy, when it is between five and six months old. You will be able to know when your queen is on heat when she becomes vocal and lies on the floor as if presenting herself to a male.

Your queen's gestation period is between 60 and 65 days. The last week of pregnancy will see your queen look for the most appropriate place to give birth. It will look for a dark yet safe place to give forth its litter. Like Abyssinians, Ocicats give birth to a few litters. Your queen will most likely give birth to three or four litters.

Building a Cattery

It is only appropriate that you build a cattery once you have established yourself as an Ocicat breeder. A cattery is where you house your cats for commercial purpose. Although yours will be a breeding cattery, you will also have the option of using it as a boarding cattery in which case other cat owners not able to travel with their cats will bring their cats to you for safe keeping at a fee.

It is mandatory that you apply for a license from your local authority before you can build a cattery. You also need to follow cattery building guidelines provided by a registry you register with. Every registry has minimum cattery construction requirements that you must stick to before you can receive another license from the registrar. A registrar will only grant you a cattery license after inspecting your cattery and certifying it to have met the set minimum construction requirements. Most registrars engage the service of local veterinarians to undertake search inspections. It will be the responsibility of the appointed vet to inspect your cattery on a regular basis to ensure that you stick to set breeding guidelines.

There are several minimum requirements when it comes to constructing a cattery, one of which being space. Your cattery needs to be spacious enough to accommodate all your cats comfortably. The minimum space per cat is set at 30 cubic feet. In addition, you need to create a space for play, grooming and maintenance. Established breeders go the extra mile to group and house their stock according to their age. Groups are housed in separated cages as one way of preventing diseases.

The other very important minimum requirement you need to meet is to construct your cattery in such a way that it allows for free flow of fresh air for your cats' good health. Your cattery should not only have enough windows but large enough windows that allow for free flow of air in and out of the cattery. The fact that Ocicats are both indoor and outdoor pets makes it very necessary that you have windows that allow a sufficient amount of light into the cattery. Artificial lighting may be necessary to achieve this if the windows do not provide for sufficient light.

Cat registrars are very strict when it comes to cattery sanitation. Not only are you required to construct your cattery in a clean environment; you will also need to ensure that there is high a standard of cleanliness in and around your cattery on a daily basis. Sanitation is one of the most important things that an appointed veterinarian will always pay attention to whenever he/she pays a visit to your cattery.

Such guidelines are not only requirements, they are mandatory taking into account the fact that failure to observe them can lead to the occurrence of cat diseases that can wipe out your cat population. Apart from such guidelines, you will need to have all the necessary supplies and equipment that your cats will need for good health and play activities. You will also need to engage the service of a veterinarian who will be available whenever the situation demands and when it is time for vaccinations.

Chapter 16 – International & National Cat Organizations, Associations & Clubs

There are many international and national organizations, associations and clubs that are in the business of promoting and maintaining the welfare of specific cat breeds including the Ocicat breed. Most of the international and national organizations and associations are indeed cat registries. Cat clubs in particular are of special mention because they limit themselves to specific cat breeds, including the Ocicat breed. Most clubs happen to be established by cat owners. Below are just a few of the notable organizations, associations and clubs.

The American Cat Fanciers Association (ACFA)
Founded in 1955, ACFA serves the interest of cat breeders, cat owners, exhibitors and the general public in different ways. The association largely engages in promoting welfare, providing education, knowledge and enhancing the interest of domesticated cats, both purebred and non-purebred.

Membership to ACFA is open to all including members of the public with an interest in cats. Members receive several benefits including a copy of the association's regularly published ACFA bulletin that is published seven times in a year. Members also have access to many cat articles on the association's website and articles written by professional cat breeders and vets. Membership to ACFA also entitles one to vote in the association's yearly elections. Members have the obligation to elect from among themselves who to represent them in the association's board of directors. ACFA is also a cat registry that you can register your litters with as a breeder at a massive discount.

ACFA organizes cat shows at different locations in the USA, an activity that gives cat owners including Ocicat owners an opportunity to show-case their pets and possibly win show awards.

The Cat Fanciers' Association (CFA)

Founded in 1906 in the USA, CFA is the world's largest cat registry of pedigree cats. Headquartered in Ohio, the association has a mission to preserve and promote pedigree breeds of cats with the aim of enhancing their well-being. CFA current cat breed registration stands at 43 including the Ocicat breed. CFA has witnessed unprecedented growth since 2006 after its centennial celebrations, growth that has seen the association recognize 39 breeds for its Championship Class.

In addition to registering cat breeds, CFA also offers several other services to purebred cat owners, catteries and the general public. It has registered cat pedigrees that date back three generations.

Perhaps one of the most memorable moments for CFA was in 1994 when it hosted the CFA International Cat Show, the largest in USA cat shows. In addition to organizing cat shows, CFA is also engaged in setting and enforcing cat breed standards through cattery inspections, training cat show judges, supporting and publicizing research on cat issues, influencing cat legislation agendas and running cat breed rescue programs.

The Cat Owner's Association of Western Australia (COAWA)

Founded in 1992 in Western Australia, COAWA exists as a cat registry and an advisory body to the Coordinating Cat Council of Australia. COAWA registers pedigree cats and provides a platform where cat breeders, cat owners and members of the public meet. It also registers non-pedigree cats.

In addition to cat breed registration, COAWA also organizes cat shows including kitten and adult championship shows. The association currently has four cat clubs affiliated to it and boasts a good number of cat breed judges.

The Governing Council of the Cat Fancy (GCCF)
Founded in 1910, GCCF is the largest cat registry in the UK. It largely registers pedigree cats. GCCF was founded by smaller cat registries and is now an independent council with over 150 member clubs including Ocicat clubs across the UK. In addition to being a cat registry, GCCF also licenses cat shows organized by all cat clubs affiliated to it. It currently licenses over 100 cat shows every year. Apart from licensing cat shows organized by its clubs, GCCF also organizes its own cat show dubbed the Supreme Cat Show, which is usually the largest cat show in the world.

The International Cat Association (TICA)
TICA is the world's largest single cat association. Its membership comprises of catteries, cat owners and people interested in cats. Based in the USA, TICA draws its membership from across the globe including from Africa, Latin America, North America, Europe and Asia. It is a cat genetic registry that also registers new cat breeds. In addition to registering pedigree cat breeds, TICA also registers non-pedigree household cats that enjoy the same status as pedigree cats in terms of cat shows and awards.

In an effort to enhance cat breeding, TICA has an elaborate Junior Exhibition specially tailored for children who love cats, giving them a good opportunity to graduate to senior levels as cat breeders.

TICA has clear responsibilities that include the registration of both pedigree and non-pedigree litters, formulation of regulations for management of cat associations, licensing of cat shows organized by its members, establishing cat breed standards, dissemination of cat breed information, organization of cat exhibitions and education of cat owners among other responsibilities.

World Pet Association (WPA)
WPA is a body that exists to bring pet food manufacturers and pet owners together. It allows for the two parties to interact through education and the sharing of information. Most of its members happen to be cat food manufacturers, cat breeders, cat organizations and associations. WPA is basically the cat industry's premier trade association. It plays a very important role in disseminating information, educating and supporting research related to cat food.

World Cat Congress (WCC)
WCC is a confederation of the largest international and national cat organizations and associations. It exists to promote understanding and cooperation among all the organizations and associations on matters that concern them. It encourages international cooperation among its membership on such matters as veterinary issues, legislations, pedigree issues and other related matters. Its membership includes FIFE, CFA, TICA, WCF, ACF, GCCF and NZCF among many other international and national organizations/associations.

Joining any of these organizations/associations provides for several benefits, particularly if you wish to be an Ocicat breeder. Such benefits include breed information, breed standards and general breeding information. You also get the opportunity to take part in many international and national cat shows and championships organized in different regions across the world throughout any given year. Joining any of the organizations also gives you a good opportunity to become a cat judge at cat shows and championships; the ultimate dream of many cat breeders and dedicated cat owners.

Conclusion

Cats and Ocicats in particular make very good pets. Not only is the Ocicat beautiful but also very adorable. You will never feel bored when living with an Ocicat. It is a playful cat that engages you all the time. It will always want you to give it attention, which is perfectly normal since it may be the only trusted companion you can have at home.

The Ocicat is a cat that does not discriminate when it comes to family members. It is particularly very good with children, to whom it develops a very strong bond because of its playful nature. Furthermore, the cat is very receptive to training.

According to research studies published in the Journal of Vascular and Interventional Neurology, living with a cat provides for several health benefits. One of the main benefits is that living with a cat reduces the risk of suffering from cardiovascular diseases including heart attack. Other health benefits associated with living with a cat include reduced risk of high stress level, reduced cholesterol level and reduced risk of depression.

Children raised in an environment where there is a cat have also been noted to grow up healthier than those raised in an environment where there is none. Unlike most cat breeds, the Ocicat breed is very cost effective. It is generally a healthy breed that is less susceptible to common diseases that other cat breeds are highly susceptible to. The fact that the breed's kittens do not inherit serious diseases/health conditions translates into reduced veterinary expenses.

The popularity of the Ocicat across the globe is not in doubt. It is one of the top cat breeds that most home owners prefer to have in their homes as indoor and outdoor pets. Its' popularity is also evident in the increasing number of cat breeders registering with different cat registries around the world. It is also not surprising that dedicated Ocicat clubs are also being established in different regions around the world.

You can choose to have two Ocicats as indoor and outdoor pets or join the big league as an Ocicat breeder. While you will have a loyal, lovely, obedient and a valuable companion if you choose to have them as pets, you are also most likely to excel as a breeder should you decide to go that route.

Published by IMB Publishing 2014

Made in the USA
San Bernardino, CA
01 February 2020

63889798R00084